Wishing Upon A Star

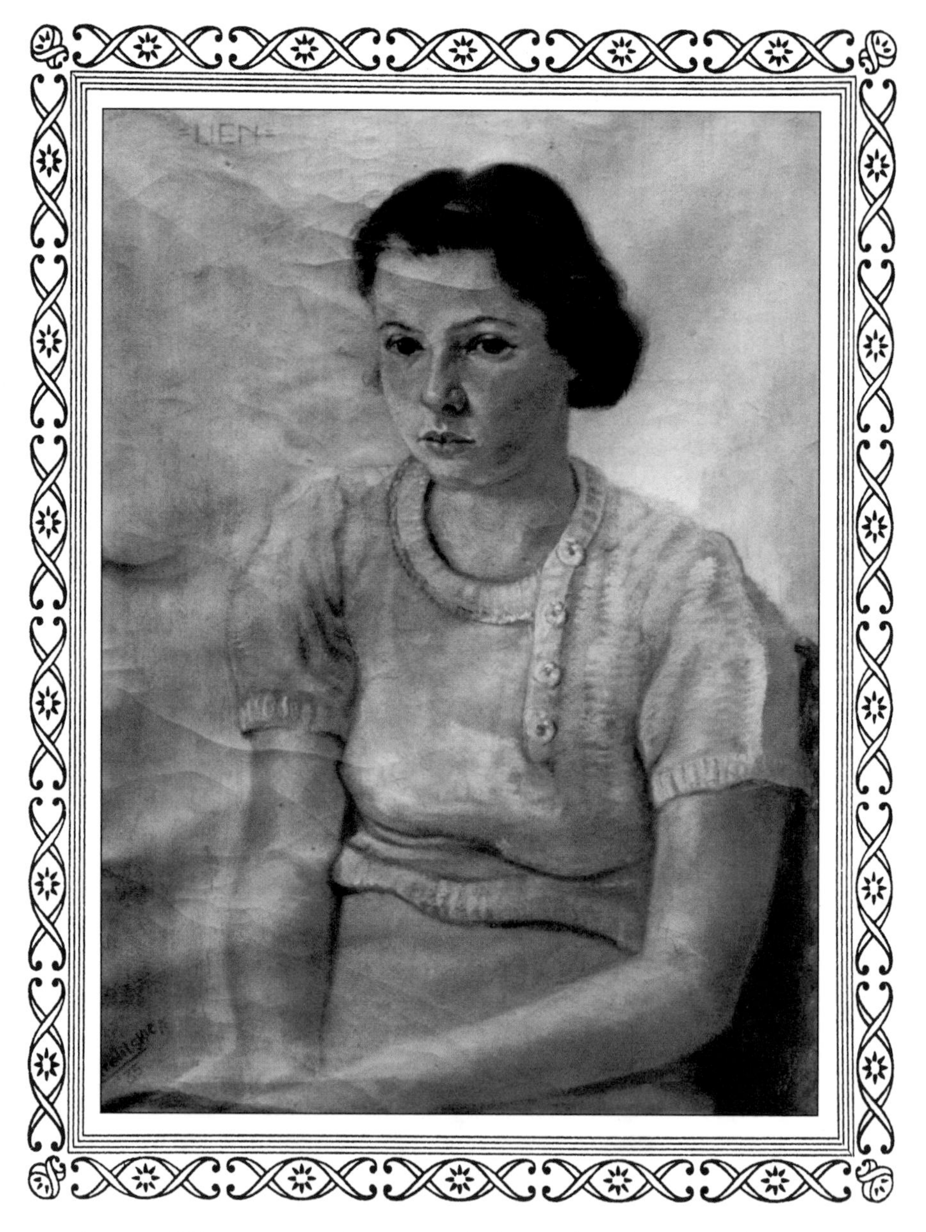

Portrait of Eline at age twelve painted by her uncle, Eddie Strelitskie – 1935

(Portrait photographed by Anton Dresden)

8/28/04

To: Chava Leah

Eline Hoekstra-Dresden

Wishing Upon A Star

A Tale of the Holocaust and Hope

Eline Hoekstra Dresden

Edited by Judi Thompson & Faith Yang
with a foreword by Marshall Lee

Oregon City, Oregon

WISHING UPON A STAR

Printed in the United States of America

Book Design by Judi Thompson
Cover Artwork by Faith Yang
Typesetting by Michele Lubke, Admiral Typesetting
Portland, Oregon
Printing by Cascade Printing, Corvallis, Oregon

ISBN 0-9714278-0-1

Previously Published by

Bearing Truth Publishing
Oregon City, Oregon
EHOEKDRES@juno.com
(503)656-2461

*May the souls of those who vanished shine
in the firmament as an eternal beacon against
inhumanity, arrogance, prejudice and hate.*

In Remembrance...

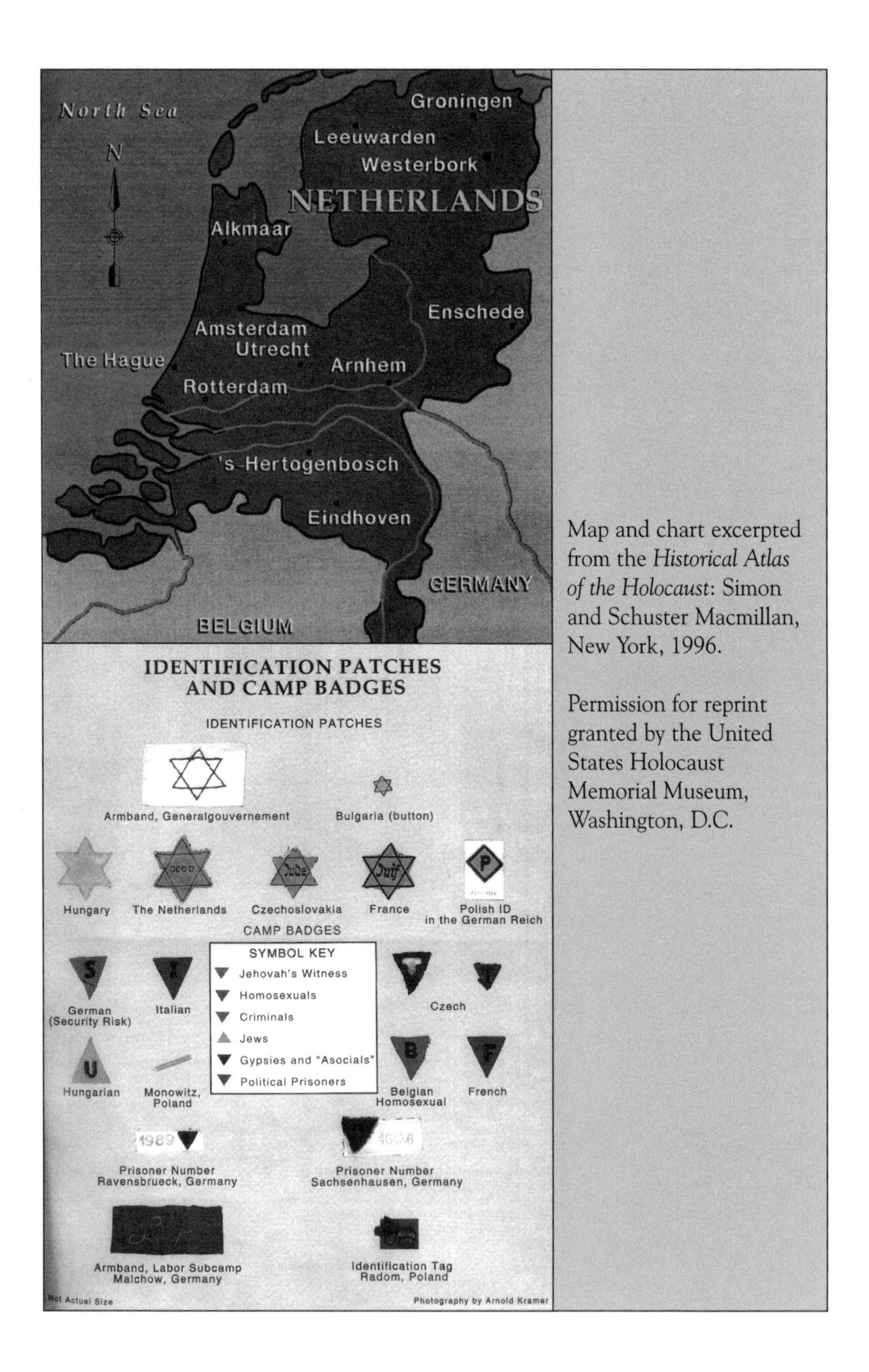

Map and chart excerpted from the *Historical Atlas of the Holocaust*: Simon and Schuster Macmillan, New York, 1996.

TABLE OF CONTENTS

ACKNOWLEDGEMENTS

First of all my sincere thanks to every one of my children and grandchildren for giving me the confidence to further develop a short account of events that happened before they were born and which made a mark on their lives.

A big thank you to my granddaughter Keesje who put my handwritten first draft in type, correcting many grammar mistakes.

I want to express my appreciation to many co-workers and friends who encouraged me in telling the story.

I want to mention Sandy Glover, Reference Librarian of the West Linn Public Library, who helped me so much in my research.

My brother Tony who did such a good job on the pictures.

Of course, a big thank you goes to my editor Judi Thompson (my publisher Blackmore and Blackmore) who led me by the hand, all the way!

Last and not least, my admiration and sincere thank you to my daughter-in-law Faith Yang, who spent numerous hours on editing and research from the time it became obvious we were committed to publishing.

FOREWORD

by Marshall M. Lee

Between 1939 and 1945 the murderous tide of the Holocaust engulfed virtually all of Europe, from deep in Soviet Russia in the east to the Atlantic coast of France in the west. Tragically, the events that had overtaken Jews in Germany since 1933 soon overwhelmed the Jews of occupied Europe. World War II began on September 1, 1939, with Germany's invasion of Poland. Within the next two years Germany conquered Poland, Denmark, Norway, The Netherlands, Belgium, France, Luxembourg, Yugoslavia, and Greece. By September 1941, German troops in North Africa had entered Egypt, threatening the Suez Canal and the entire Middle East. In Russia that same September, the German army prepared for what her generals believed would be the final offensive on Moscow and the capitulation of the Soviet Union. And in every city, in every town, in every *shtetl* conquered by the Germans, Jews were at risk, for even as the German army passed through a town, behind the front line troops came other soldiers, sometimes regular army, sometimes police units, more often the dreaded S.S., whose mission it was to find and eventually to murder every single Jew they could find. But why the Jews?

When Adolf Hitler became chancellor of Germany in 1933, the National Socialists quickly consolidated their power, eliminating all opposition and establishing Hitler's dictatorship over Germany. At the core of Hitler's worldview and of the Nazis' political program was the belief that German citizenship was defined by race, or "blood" as the Nazis claimed. Only those with "pure blood" could be considered members of Germany's "people's community." Ominously, the Nazis defined the purity of German blood by the absence of "Jewish blood." Jews, it seemed, represented a threat to Germany's racial purity, since according to Hitler and the Nazis the blood of the racially inferior Jews threatened "to pollute" Germany's racial stock. Far too few Germans stopped to question the logic or the morality of Hitler's racial politics, according to which Jews, whose historical culture and ethnicity were defined by their religion, now saw their religion determine their biological identity. This mixture of religion and biology became the law of the land in Germany in 1935 with the Nuremberg Laws, according to which Germany's Jews were deprived of their citizenship because of their "Jewish blood."

To Germans, indeed to many throughout Europe, the Nazis' attack on German Jews had a certain appeal. Hitler and the Nazis, as well as others on the political right, capitalized on the widespread public fear and resentment of economic, political and social turmoil in the years after Germany's defeat in World War I. With the onset of the Great Depression in 1929, conditions throughout Europe deteriorated still more dramatically, creating the environment in which Hitler and the Nazis could flourish. Their most powerful appeal: that the public's suffering was the result of a Jewish conspiracy; that not only in Germany but globally, Jews had secretly plotted to take over the world. It was Germany's destiny, according to Hitler, that she rebuild herself and wage a victorious crusade against this international Jewish conspiracy. And this proved powerfully appealing to those who longed to blame someone or something else for their own suffering. The Jews proved to be the ideal scapegoat.

Thus it was that in Germany the appeal of National Socialism had so much to do with anti-Semitism. Thus it was that by 1939, half of Germany's Jews had left their native country, while those who remained lived in virtual exile in their own country, deprived of civil rights, property rights, and the right to practice their chosen professions. Vilified by relentless Nazi propaganda, German Jews existed in the eyes of the state not as human beings but as objects. And it was as objects that German authorities viewed the Jews of occupied Europe once World War II began. Ultimately, within the compass of German conquest and occupation, some ten million Jews would come under German control. From 1939 to 1945, the organized murder of Europe's Jews, known by the Germans as the "Final Solution of the Jewish Question," claimed more than five million Jews.

The highest concentration of Jews in Europe was found in Eastern Europe, specifically Poland and Soviet Russia, and there in the East, German anti-Jewish policy reached its most barbaric zenith. In Poland, the Ukraine and Russia Nazi authorities envisioned a vast colonial empire of German settlers. According to Nazi racial doctrine, not only were Jews to be killed, but the native Slavic peoples of the East were expendable, the chattel of their German overlords. At first German forces simply rounded up the Jews of Poland, the Baltic States, the Ukraine and Russia, and shot them. These shooting actions, at first conducted by the infamous *Einsatzgruppen*, grew in scope to include police units and elements of the regular army, and claimed roughly 1.25 million Jews in Eastern Europe between the summer of 1941 and the end of 1942. By mid-1942, however, the Germans began to switch their murder operations from mobile killing actions in the field to industrially organized murder in stationary killing centers established at six camps in Poland and Upper Silesia: Chelmno, Sobibor, Treblinka, Belzec, Majdanek and Auschwitz/Birkenau. At these six killing centers the Germans used poison gas to kill their victims, who arrived by train from the ghettoes of Poland, and from further afield.

On January 22, 1942, at a villa on the shore of the Wannsee, a suburban lake on the outskirts of Berlin, German officials met to implement the organizational details of the Final Solution. Under the leadership of the S.S., civilian and military agencies coordinated their efforts with the S.S. for the identification, arrest and transportation of Jews from every corner of occupied Europe to "the East," to the killing centers of Poland and Upper Silesia. Among the reasons for such detailed planning and coordination was the fact that German occupation authorities in Western Europe realized that the Jews of Belgium, Denmark, France, Holland and Norway were more fully assimilated into society, and therefore more difficult to round up and deport. In Western Europe, moreover, the Germans feared that the civil population would be less tolerant of German efforts to round up Jews. Thus it would be necessary to create a process that would extract the Jews from society, relocate them to transit centers and thence transport them, to be disposed of at one of the killing center camps in the East.

In the end, experiences varied. On the one hand, when the Germans came for Denmark's 7,500 Jews in October of 1943 the Danish resistance smuggled 7,000 to Sweden during a spectacular three-week operation. The Germans managed to deport the remaining 500 with the intention of sending them to Auschwitz and certain death.

So intense was the interest of the Danish government in the fate of these 500 Danish Jews and so persistent were the Danes' queries, however, that the Germans never did transport them to Auschwitz. These 500 Danes remained at the Theresienstadt camp in Bohemia until the end of the war.

While Denmark's example remains unparalleled in the history of the Holocaust, that of France is less reassuring. When France surrendered to Germany in June 1940, there were some 300,000 Jews in France. German troops occupied northern and western France, while central and southern France remained under French administration by the collaborationist Vichy government. The Germans enlisted the help of the Vichy authorities and other collaborationists, enabling them to round up and deport some 75,000 Jews from France between June 1940 and August 1944. Again with the help of their French collaborators, the Germans set up a system of twenty-six camps in France for the internment and transit of Jews to the camps of Poland and Upper Silesia. On the other hand, the various arms of the French resistance, as well as individual French citizens, intervened to shelter and to save Jews, often at great personal risk. Indeed, one of the single most remarkable episodes of rescue during the Holocaust occurred in Le Chambon sur Ligne in southeastern France, where the entire town transformed itself into a refuge for Jews. Under the leadership of their pastor, André Trocmé and his wife Magda, the intensely religious Protestant Chambonnais followed the dictates of their conscience and of the New Testament, understanding that to fail to help those in need would in fact be an act of harm. In this way, with no fanfare, the people of Le Chambon sheltered and saved hundreds of Jews from their Vichy pursuers.

If Denmark represents the most admirable civic response to Germany's war against the Jews, and France a mixture of rescue and betrayal, The Netherlands represents perhaps the most troubling case in Western Europe. On May 10, 1940, Germany invaded Belgium, Luxembourg and The Netherlands, all three of which had been neutral since Germany's invasion of Poland and the declaration of war with France and Great Britain at the beginning of September 1939. Within days of Germany's invasion, the Dutch government surrendered and the people of Holland found themselves occupied by German troops and at the mercy of Arthur Seyss-Inquart, the governor-general of occupied Holland. Elsewhere in Western Europe – France, Belgium, Denmark – the German occupation was under the *Wehrmacht*, the German Army, but in Holland things were different. Since the Dutch people appeared to the Nazis to be so similar in their racial character, Berlin aimed to integrate Holland into Germany proper at some later date. It seemed appropriate to Berlin, then, to administer The Netherlands in a more intimate way, to allow the Nazi Party to prepare the way for integration into Germany proper. At the head of this Nazi Party occupation of Holland was Arthur Seyss-Inquart, prominent Nazi Party member and former Nazi Party leader in Austria.

From the outset the occupation of Holland imposed anti-Jewish measures on the Dutch, and since Dutch authorities labored under the zealous eyes of Nazi Party officials, these measures were vigorously applied. In January 1941, the Germans ordered the 160,000 Jews in Holland to register with the local authorities, thereby self-identifying themselves. All told, some 140,000 Jews reported. Part of this identification process required Jews to wear the yellow Star of David on their clothing as a way of making Jews conspicuously obvious to the authorities and to any passerby. As part of their offensive, the Germans established two camps in Holland: Vught in the south, and Westerbork in Drente to the north. From these camps began deportations in 1942, deportations that continued for two years, until the fall of 1944, and which claimed more than seventy-five percent of Holland's Jews.

There are cases of Jews hidden and saved by families and individuals in Holland. But these cases were too few. What has shocked scholars and survivors since the Holocaust is how thorough was the roundup of Jews in Holland, how frequently Jews were betrayed, and what a disproportionate number of Jews from The Netherlands perished in the Holocaust. Virtually everyone today is familiar with the story of Anne Frank, who with her family and others went into hiding in Amsterdam in the summer of 1942. Betrayed in August of 1944, the Franks were sent to Westerbork and from there east to Auschwitz. Of the Frank family only Otto, Anne's father, survived. The Franks' experience in some ways encapsulates that of Jews in Holland, for not only were they hidden by courageous Christian friends, they were betrayed by others, and indeed those who came to arrest the Franks included members of the Dutch constabulary.

The Franks' tragic story is one of unyielding hope, as two families struggled to stay together amidst the most harrowing conditions. The story of Eline Hoekstra Dresden is a similar story, a story of hope, of luck, of survival. The remarkable fact of her family's survival may tempt the reader into feelings of false satisfaction. After all, Eline survived, as did her immediate family, as did her fiancé and infant son. But none survived without hardship; even the infant Daantje who lived in hiding was deprived of his mother for three years. Whatever happy ending tempts the reader, remember this: the single determining factor in the survival of this family was luck. Remember, too, the reality they faced at war's end was the emptiness of their survival: no grandparents, not one aunt, not one uncle, not one cousin were there to greet them. This, rather than their survival, is the legacy of the Holocaust. How fortunate we are, then, to have the handful of survivors like Eline to tell us how it was.

Marshall M. Lee, Ph.D.

Distinguished Professor of History (ret.)
Director, Oregon Holocaust
Resource Center (ret.)
Pacific University
June 2000

PROLOGUE

Hope is one ingredient needed for survival, but it does not guarantee it. Because of my experiences, I have thought a lot about this concept of Hope. I believe it can be defined in many ways. It is faith in a higher power or in a guardian angel you can call upon when in need. It is the faith of the gambler believing his lucky number will come up. It is the ability to accumulate experience on which to build. It is the catalyst for our expectations of the future, based upon positive outcomes in life. Perhaps it is an innate quality that insures survival of the species. I have wondered if it is something which we learn in order to stay positive and optimistic, or perhaps it is the ability to visualize a good outcome. Perhaps it is the belief that there is a way to influence the future by convincing ourselves that there is such a thing as "good luck."

Sometimes I think that Hope is the belief that by relying on our own strength we can control the course of events by using the power of our minds. At other times I think it is the result of having personal resources so well-organized and practiced that we can instantly access them when needed. And I wonder if it is the manifestation of a connection we have with loved ones who have been in similar circumstances. However we define it, I think Hope is an instinctive quality without which we would quickly succumb to destruction through adversity.

I am seventy-seven and semi-retired. When I was asked to write down my memories I dismissed the idea because I am not a writer. My life was fated to take me through an historically important time. I decided, however, that my stories might show others that the dangerous theories and beliefs denying the Holocaust are false. Perhaps I could make people aware of the value of not giving up hope, of retaining a sense of humor, and of stretching one's physical and emotional strengths always a little further, even to their limits.

I realize that my generation – the adults of World War II – will soon be gone. The Holocaust made an indelible mark on my being. I am grateful that I survived and so very fortunate that my husband and son survived as well. I want my grandchildren and great-grandchildren to be interested in the history of their ancestors. These writings will explain some of the psychological difficulty that I still experience, such as the occasional sudden panic, partially caused by my war experiences.

In the book, *The Holocaust: The Fate of European Jewry*, Leni Yahil, a history professor at the University of Haifa, wrote about the passage to the gas chambers at Auschwitz, as told by a camp survivor at the trial of Adolf Eichmann:

The people came through the infamous Himmelstrasse, which led from Camp 1 to Camp 2. Standing in the Himmelstrasse were S.S. men with dogs, whips and clubs. The people walked quietly: that was at the beginning, in the summer of 1942. They didn't know where they were headed for. When they entered the gas chambers, two Ukrainians were standing by the door...They provided the gas...The last people to enter the gas chambers were pricked with bayonets, since they could see what was going on inside and didn't want to enter. Four hundred people were placed in the small gas chamber...so that they barely managed to close the chamber's outer door. When they did close it, we were on the other side. Then we heard the shouts: "Hear O Israel!" "Papa!" "Mama!" Within thirty-five minutes they were dead. Two Germans stood listening to what was happening inside. Finally, they said, "They're all asleep." They told [us] to open the door. We opened the door and removed the corpses.

Professor Yahil further describes the address of Hans Rauter, (the Commissioner of Public Security in Holland), to his team on March 22, 1943, in which he said, "I intend to remove the Jews as fast as possible. This is not a pleasant task. It is dirty work. But it is a step of great historical importance. We cannot even guess what it means to cast out from the body of a nation 120,000 Jews who within a century might have reached one million. What we are doing for the benefit of the body of people must be done without mercy, and there is no room for softness and weakness... We only want to recover from this distress and the Jewish problem must be clarified finally and conclusively."

By the war's end, 110,000 Jews had been deported from Holland. Five thousand returned. Thirty-five thousand Dutch Jews survived. 105,000 Jews were killed; that is, seventy percent of the Dutch Jewish population, the highest loss of Jews from any one country, except Poland.

My two-year imprisonment began in the castle "De Schaffelaar" in Barneveld, a small city in the center of The Netherlands, during the occupation by the Germans. It ended at Camp Westerbork near Hooghalen in the northeastern part of The Netherlands close to the German border. I was spared the death camps and never knew about the gas chambers and crematoria in Auschwitz, or any of the terrible tortures and killings going on in the hundreds of other concentration camps in Germany and Poland.

I wonder why I am not overcome with emotion as I put all of this on paper. Sometimes it seems as if something is missing, as if the pain is buried too deep to emerge. I accept this because the detachment makes it easier to remember details and to translate my experiences into sentences with a precision that will paint a sharp picture of the suffering of so many people, the unreal, nightmarish existence, the humiliation, the complete absence of a normal life, and the fear. Fear was always with me, functioning as a shield, almost a dear companion. I was afraid to not be afraid. It may seem an odd way to protect oneself, but it did not feel odd then. Even though we thought we could run from the danger, we were never sure which way to go. It reminds me of how a fugitive can feel relief, in some way, when finally caught; but for those who were interned as Jews, the emotion of relief was non-existent; it quickly became apparent that other, much more painful things were in store, so the sense of endangerment was never-ending. Fear and the desire to survive were the only constants.

Millions wished upon a star. Willing to suffer abuse, hunger and hard labor, they wished for their lives and the lives of their loved ones to be spared. They did not have the slightest idea that annihilation was waiting, but an instinctive fear and feeling of doom was universal among them. Did the world, watching the same stars at night, hear their pleas and yet do nothing to stop the tragedy? The stars the Jews wished upon brought only misery, pain and death. They wore them on their clothes, marked as ones to be herded and destroyed by a "master race" along with thousands of gypsies, homosexuals, and disabled people. The Nazis did not kill millions of people in cold blood but rather in hot boiling blood, powered by a perverse passion to see these unfortunate lives writhing in despair.

Chapter 1

HOW I GREW UP

I was born in 1923 in The Netherlands in The Hague, a beautiful large city with many fountains and a deer park in the center of town. I was the youngest of the four children of Daniel Dresden and Mietje Dresden Strelitskie. The oldest child was a boy, Daniel; then a year later came Anton ("Tony"), and a year after came my sister, Mimi. Six years after that, I was born. We were a middle-class family. I am told that everyone spoiled me, but I certainly didn't see it as a problem. My father was a professor at the University of Delft, teaching on the subjects of pumps and turbines. He decided to leave when he felt that the faculty was not supporting his efforts by denying his department the laboratory he had requested. I am sure that stubbornness played a role in his decision.

The Hague is about fifteen kilometers from the popular beach resort, Scheveningen, where we went to play. The name "Scheveningen" is very difficult for most native Germans to pronounce correctly, and so during the occupation of The Netherlands in World War II, it was used as a test to determine whether a person was really Dutch or a German posing as Dutch.

Eline with her mother and brothers, Tony and Daniel

Scheveningen, 1925

When I was six years old, we moved to Utrecht where my father became the technical director of a turbine factory. We lived in a comfortable three-story house with hardwood floors and a wood or gas stove in each room. We rented because it was not common to own a house unless one was rich. Behind the front door with its beveled glass inset was the vestibule, a large space with a swinging glass door that led to the hallway. The vestibule served as a trap for cold air and as a receiving place for visitors. Beyond that was an atrium with a marble floor and in the center was a large coal-burning stove with a pipe that went straight up to the roof and served as a heating column for the whole house. It had to be filled through a large opening on the top while a grate on the bottom could be shaken to let the ashes fall into an ash-drawer. On the top of the stove was a cover shaped like a crown with the same ornamental pattern on the feet. It stood on a marble slab and was attended to day and night. I thought of it as the warm heart of the house. A large winding staircase led to the upper stories. All of the doors had raised oak thresholds to keep out cold air. Every one of the fifteen rooms in the house was put to use. As a child, I used to play with three balls on the landing of the staircase leading to the second story. Looking back, I now realize what gracious living this was, although I didn't know it at the time.

Mimi, Mother, Eline and Marie ("Plie")

The Hague, 1924

The kitchen was large with a smooth granite floor that was scrubbed every day. The countertops were made of zinc that curved up to form a backsplash. Every Saturday they had to be cleaned and shined with a paste made from powdered chalk and lemon. The kitchen walls were painted blue because it was thought that this color kept the flies away. I often wondered if this was the reason that Delft tiles were blue. A large wood stove for cooking sat next to the gas range. The woven mats on the floor were swatted every day to clean them, but I didn't pay much attention to all of this hard work since we had two live-in helpers.

The people who worked for us were all non-Jews. Marie, the oldest, was like a surrogate mother as my own mother was gone most of the time doing volunteer work. Marie was seventeen when she came to us and I was one year old. When I started talking, I pronounced her name as "Plie" and the name stuck. She listened to my stories after school and gave me the heels of the fresh loaves of bread that were delivered every day at seven o'clock in the morning. Mother planned the weekly menus but Plie did the shopping and took care of most of the household management. The younger helper, Joop (pronounced "Yope"), was a tall, voluptuous, fun-loving girl with long blonde hair. Joop was in charge of the housekeeping; she cleaned the rooms and aired the bedding daily. This airing was necessary because in those days, we did not bathe or change clothes every day. In the spring and fall we had a seamstress who lived with us for a week, sewing new clothes for the next season. We had subscriptions to theaters and concerts. I did not get to go very often, but my brothers and sister were old enough to appreciate these things and thus received a cultural education.

The household staff ate in the kitchen at a big table placed against a wall with a little window that was used to pass dishes through to the dining room. This kept cooking odors confined to the kitchen and facilitated the return of the dirty dishes as well. I spent many happy hours in the kitchen with Marie, Joop, and the part-time helpers who were young girls who cleaned stoops, windows, and floors, polished the silver and washed vegetables. Meat, vegetables and bread were ordered early in the morning and were delivered to the house by merchants. Vendors with horse-drawn carts came every two weeks, selling household articles such as brushes or shoe polish. Housewives would come outside to make their choices and visit with each other at the same time. I played in the large back yard with its gravel pathway, flowerbeds and grass, surrounded by oak trees, birches, and Douglas fir. For fun, I would bounce balls against the side of the house or search for pretty rocks in the gravel. A sixty-foot raised verandah hugged the width of the house. It was made of red tile with brick walls and steps that led to the paths in the yard and was often used for dining or afternoon tea with family and guests. Access to it was through the family and dining rooms by way of large French doors that swung out. The verandah was covered by an awning that creaked when raised or lowered with a crank. Each winter, carpenters took it down and put it in storage.

We lived in this big house until 1938 when we moved to a house that my father bought at *Konigslaan* 80. It faced the beautiful Wilhelmina Park, named after the Queen of Holland. This house was newly built and very comfortable, with central heating and a modern kitchen. The front yard was very small, but there was a fair-sized backyard with a back

Mother, Eline, Daniel, Mimi and Tony

The Hague, 1927

entrance lane that we used to get to a shed where we stored our bicycles. I missed the large older house with its romantic nooks and crannies, but it was quite an occasion to own a house instead of renting one. In our new place we had one less maid, so the sheets and table linens were sent out to be laundered. They came back in neat little stacks held together with a narrow, flat blue string tied in a bow. The dirty laundry was stored in the cellar in a big blue crate with a chicken-wire lid to allow it to air.

Eline

The Hague, 1928

Plie got married the year of the move. She continued to work for us, but lived with her husband a few streets away. When she became pregnant it was decided she was going to deliver the baby in our home because it was larger and since a normal birth was expected, there was no need to go to a hospital. I well remember the night she gave birth. Since she was so loved by all of us, we sat on the stairs leading to the "delivery room," situating ourselves to hear the first cries of the baby, a healthy little boy.

In the summer we often went to the coast in Zeeland on the southwestern tip of Holland and stayed in a pension similar to a bed-and-breakfast, but with dinner included. Guests sat together at large community tables, which made for interesting conversations. Father took all of us children on hiking trips and sometimes we camped overnight. During my teen years our family had a car, usually a big touring car such as a Fiat or Studebaker. I remember a convertible with a heavy cloth top that had to be put up and pulled down by hand. It snapped onto the chassis at the sides and it had mica windows, as plastic was not yet common. Father bought these cars used and registered them for use only in the summers when we took vacations. We went to Paris, camping on

Left to right: Eline's brother Tony, Mimi, Eline and her brother, Daniel at the beach in Domberg.

1928

Daniel, Cousin Anton, Mother, Eline, Father, Mimi and Tony posing in traditional dress on vacation.

1928

the way, or to Switzerland or Italy, and sometimes the car would break down on a trip. One time this happened when we were close to the Fiat factory in Milan and so we waited in a hotel while the transmission was repaired. My father had to pay for accommodations for nine people!

I almost felt as if I were an only child because my siblings were already teenagers when I was in grade school. I didn't like school very much. For the first six years, I was in a Montessori school. My parents thought this was an excellent educational system and my brothers and sister went there too. Montessori emphasizes individualism and independence, two traits I already had in abundance. Later, when I went to public school I spent a lot of time in the principal's office because I had gotten accustomed to the freedom of the Montessori system. I often got into trouble for disrupting the class with too many questions or too much talking and giggling. I went to a private high school where I continued to have trouble accepting discipline and regimentation; however, I got along better there because it was less traditional and the teachers had more experience with difficult children. My siblings also had a lot of trouble in the public high schools in Utrecht; in fact, both brothers were kicked out for not fitting in.

I didn't socialize much but I did read whatever I could get my hands on, often in bed under the blankets with a flashlight. I was nearsighted and wore black-rimmed glasses with legs that curved all the way around my ears and peeked out from under my earlobes. Some kids called me a "spectacle Jew." I asked my parents why some people didn't like Jews and they said that hatred was as old as time itself. They told me that I should not be scared because no one would hurt me if I did my best to be a good person. Being a good person meant following the Ten Commandments to the best of one's ability. My father said, "When you can do all that perfectly, then you can worry about loving your neighbors." I remember my father as being fair, loving, understanding and patient. He was always someone who would take the time to listen. Even now, thirty-five years after his death, thinking about him makes me feel good.

I met my future husband, Kees, in the private school. He had lived in Surinam for three years, from the ages of eleven to fourteen, where his father was a minister. Surinam was one of several Dutch colonies which included the West Indies, Curacao, Aruba, and the East Indies, including Sumatra and Java, among others. These countries mainly had grade schools; high schools were rare. Many parents who had careers in the colonies had to send their children to Holland for high school and college.

A few could afford private teachers but then the children missed out on social opportunities. "The curse of the tropics" was an expression that described the necessity of sending one's teen-aged children away. Parents often paid for their children to live with families in which the father was a teacher who would help with homework. Usually the children would go home to visit once a year. Since it was often not possible to send the children to Holland at the beginning of the public school year, private schools were the alternative. Kees' parents temporarily returned to Holland in 1936. His mother died the following year and his father returned to Surinam, leaving Kees and his younger brother Johan in Holland to go to the school that I happened to be attending.

* * * * * *

Montessori Classroom
Eline is front right, in short-sleeved sweater

The Hague, 1930

In 1939, Hitler was already persecuting German and Polish Jews. Many Jewish parents were desperate to find some way of saving their children by getting them out of the country to a safe haven. The Netherlands was one of the few countries willing to accept Jewish refugees. Willing, but not eager. Two little girls named Selma and Trudie, ages five and seven, were put on a train by their parents in Germany. The girls arrived in Holland with only the clothes they wore, a small satchel with a doll for each girl, and some underwear. They were two of many children who were taken to a Jewish orphanage while the Jewish Committee tried to find homes for them. The Jewish Committee was formed mainly for the purpose of helping refugees. We had heard horror stories about the situation in Germany and my parents wanted to do something for the Jews who suffered under Hitler's regime.

Selma and Trudie arrived at our household just before I was to go on a winter sports trip to Austria with my high school. The trip was inexpensive, but still a luxury and a vacation that few could afford. My brothers and sister had been on these trips before and had told me wonderful stories about skiing, but my parents decided it would be insensitive for me to take a pleasure trip while these two unfortunate children were in our home. I was very disappointed to miss the trip I had been so eagerly anticipating, but I agreed with my parents' point of view.

It was difficult to get close to the girls. They didn't talk much and when they did, it was in German or Polish. I can still see them sitting together in a big leather chair, looking like two hurt, frightened little birds. Trudie had been told by their parents to take care of her little sister and Selma, knowing this, treated her like a slave. Trudie often wet her bed, or so we thought. We found out that Selma was actually the bed-wetter and made Trudie trade sheets to appear as though it were her sister who had the problem. In the mornings when Trudie buttoned her sister's dress, Selma would undo all the buttons and make her do it all over again. Mealtime was unpleasant because Selma would throw up on her plate and, when disciplined, would then throw up on Trudie's plate as well.

One day they received a package from their parents. It contained flour with worms, sugar with ants, and barley with mold. It was obviously food saved from their own mouths. It had been opened at the border and carelessly re-packaged so that everything was all mixed up. Perhaps a doll or toy had been taken from it. It made us feel sad.

After a couple of months, the girls began to open up a bit and things improved. Just as they began to feel at home, the German authorities demanded that they be returned to the Jewish orphanage. Since they were not Dutch citizens, they were considered refugees. My family went twice to see them in the orphanage, but on a subsequent visit we discovered they had been transported "east." We assumed that meant Germany, but we could not get any information about their destination. We never heard from them again. Neither did we hear again from their parents after receipt of the sad package. Many years later when I made a trip to Israel, I learned that they were taken to Auschwitz.

Eline

The Hague, 1926

Chapter 2

WAR AND PERSECUTION

I was seventeen years old and a senior in high school in the spring of 1940. I lived a life typical for a young girl from an upper middle class family, participating in sports, going on vacations with the family and getting by in school. To make my life complete I had a boyfriend, Kees (pronounced "Case"), who was eighteen. We always walked arm-in-arm during morning and afternoon breaks and everyone knew we were a couple. We had our future planned: we would become engaged after graduation and I would study medicine in Utrecht where there was a famous medical university and hospital. Kees would study tropical forestry in Wageningen, forty-five kilometers from Utrecht, (about twenty-nine miles). For a while, life was wonderful, carefree and full of hope.

Europe got a taste of turmoil after Germany invaded Poland with obvious plans to expand its territory. Even though this seemed very far away, we felt uneasy. In the first months of 1940, the political and military situations in Europe were becoming quite tense.

In spite of the atmosphere of apprehension, my parents, my fiancé and I went on vacation in Switzerland. Travelling with a trailer camper, we thoroughly enjoyed ourselves. After we heard rumors that the borders between Switzerland, France and Belgium would be closed, we decided to go home early.

Holland had been neutral for more than one hundred years and it seemed inconceivable for nations in Europe to fight each other. Completely unaccustomed to the concept of war, we were not afraid because the possibility of real danger never entered our minds. My father reassured us, saying that there would be no problems that could not be solved politically. It was his nature to be optimistic. We had an easy trip home with no trouble at the borders. When we arrived home, however, we found that there was serious concern about the threat of war.

In March 1940, to our surprise, Holland's military was mobilized. Fathers, sons and husbands had to leave home and report to their units.

It all seemed more like a play than reality, so unprepared were we for thinking about war; however, on the morning of May 10, 1940, it came to us. Early in the morning we saw planes in the clear sky, leaving puffs of white clouds behind them. Kees, sick with pneumonia, had been listening to the radio all night and was the first to hear the news when the queen announced that Germany had invaded our country. That first morning, many of us climbed onto the roof of our house to watch the little white puffs in the sky. After several hours we caught on to the fact that the airplanes were German and the white puffs the result of our anti-aircraft guns.

We stayed close to the radio for the next four days. It seemed that we lived only to hear the news. Rumors sprang up everywhere and it was difficult to get an accurate picture of what was happening. Events unfolded quickly, conflicting stories were published, and our way of life changed completely. We now heard anti-aircraft fire all day as Hitler pushed forward to cross the channel into England.

The third day after the invasion, heavy firing equipment was set up in the park across from our house. Soldiers sat smoking on the grass among the daisies, looking tense and scared. Cars fitted with loudspeakers drove through the streets ordering the people in our neighborhood to evacuate. Our family received the order to evacuate to my father's factory at the opposite end of town. We quickly gathered up flashlights and blankets before a truck from the factory came to get us.

We stopped to get Plie and her infant son. She had been married for about a year. When the time to evacuate came, she was still weak, and alone because her husband had been mobilized. She was glad we came to take her with us.

We found many employees at the factory before us, as well as sandwiches, mattresses, alarm clocks, and a radio. We tried to deny just how grave the situation was and comforted each other by saying, "It won't be long … we will be able to go home soon … the war will not last long." We listened to the radio, played games and tried to make it like a picnic. Plie, who could whistle beautifully, entertained us with lively songs. The queen spoke to the population and told us to show courage. The Dutch shield carries a motto, *Je maintiendrai*, meaning, "We will prevail." And we did, but only for four days.

The Dutch military tactics were antiquated. The strategy of inundating the land with water by destroying the dikes used to be an effective means of stopping enemies from entering the country, but with modern warfare this was futile. The German forces dropped paratroopers behind the flooded areas and took over airfields and bridges. Then they bombed Rotterdam, killing approximately one thousand people and flattening the center of town. Forty miles to the east, in our city of Utrecht, it rained ash as tiny pieces of burned paper floated down from the sky blown in by the wind from the fires in Rotterdam. We heard on the radio that the German forces were threatening to bomb other large cities such as Amsterdam and Utrecht.

On the first day of our "four-day" war, my mother, who was a Red Cross nurse, was called for duty. At a morning orientation meeting she was ordered to report to work that afternoon at a nearby railroad station where the first of the wounded soldiers were expected to arrive from the front. This was a small transfer station at the end of a lovely boulevard called the "*Maliebaan*." The neighborhood was rather grand with beautiful old houses and wide sidewalks. On each side of the center street there was a horse path separated from a bicycle path by large bushes and a foot path, all creating an elegant symmetry. It was through this pleasant environment that I went with my mother to the station and offered to help. I was only seventeen and had no training, but the extra hands were welcome. I served coffee to the soldiers, lit their cigarettes and tried to comfort them. Some of them were tied to gurneys and could not move. Having no idea yet of real misery, I felt happy to be of help. I imagined myself a budding Florence Nightingale and went home that first night tired and satisfied. The next morning as we were bicycling to the station, shots were fired at us from the houses on the boulevard. They sounded like firecrackers and we were not hit. The next day, when one of our friends was hit in the leg and shooting occurred at the railroad station, the war suddenly became real. The soldiers were extremely anxious and so were we. Now we had to watch out for our own physical safety. The explanation was that some Dutch citizens, collaborating with the Nazis, had taken possession of the large, beautiful houses belonging to doctors and lawyers who practiced in their homes on the *Maliebaan*. The collaborators had armed themselves and were shooting from second-story windows. The sniper fire happened at random so we never knew from what direction it would come next. There was more and more gunfire. After two days we got orders to evacuate the station.

On May 14, 1940, four days after the invasion, the queen announced the surrender of The Netherlands and the royal family fled to England. We felt abandoned and vulnerable. Morale was low. The soldiers were disillusioned and threw down their weapons. The German army in all its might and abundance of modern weaponry rolled into our small, peace-loving country.

Little did we expect the extent of the changes that were going to take place in our daily lives. We watched the German soldiers march into our towns, clean-shaven, neatly uniformed stepping in unison with their legs lifted high, straight and rigid. They looked like perfect toy soldiers. It seemed as if the whole population of Utrecht lined the streets as the troops marched in, singing songs. One could not help but admire their disciplined manner.

There were promises that no changes would occur in local or higher government. Police, utilities, and courts were to remain under Dutch control, but the Nazis took control of the radio stations. The general population quickly tried to form a resistance army. This was difficult because it was not known who the collaborators were. Although Holland had no history of being sympathetic to the Nazis, there were more collaborators than expected during the occupation. But there were also many wonderful citizens who risked their lives to keep in touch with Radio Holland, which was broadcast from London, and other courageous individuals who helped Jews and downed Allied fliers.

The leader of the Nazi Party in Holland, Anton Mussert, saw his chance to gain power. Mussert, a civil engineer, had been one of my father's students in Delft. On one occasion about a year after the takeover by the German forces, my father was traveling by train to Amsterdam with a special permit. The German police wanted to check the contents of his suitcase. In his pocket my father had a letter from Mussert, refusing a favor my father had requested on behalf of Jewish friends. When Father showed the police the signature on the letter, they apologized and did not check his suitcase, which, by the way, contained contraband such as coffee and cigarettes.

Holland capitulated about a month before our final exams in high school but this event did not interfere with our education at that time.

These exams consisted of week-long written tests in all subjects, and another week of oral examinations. After the tests the graduating students nervously waited outside the school and were called in alphabetical order to be told by a committee of examiners whether they had passed or not. If they failed they had to go back to high school for another year. Kees and I graduated at the beginning of June and got engaged. We did not have the custom of graduation ceremonies. We had the summer free before starting our studies. I enrolled in the university in Utrecht and Kees in Wageningen, as we had planned. My father gave me allowance for two sports, and I chose horseback riding and fencing. When classes started we visited each other, traveling by bicycle and alternating weekends in each city. The fall went by with relatively few changes in our way of life. We played tennis, went swimming, took bicycle trips, played chess, and visited friends. When the school year progressed and homework became heavy, we did not have as much time for the long weekend trips. We felt very uncomfortable being separated during those frightening times as the war approached.

Often during the night, Allied airplanes flew over us on their way to Germany. Kees had a duty, as did many students, to keep watch on top of the tower in Wageningen where an alarm was sounded to warn the city when bombers flew over. The concern was that even though the bombers did not intend to drop bombs here, their loads could fall when German anti-aircraft weapons hit them. The alarm started as a low tone then slowly rose in pitch, wailing up and down again for several minutes. Finally, the "all safe" signal of one long steady tone was sounded. We had frequent air-raid alarms in Utrecht also. Sometimes we had to wait for a couple of hours before the all-safe sign came.

Blackouts were required because the Allied forces flew over Holland on their way to Germany during the night and the city had to be dark. The windows of houses were blackened, streetlights were extinguished, bicyclists had to dim their lights. Even the headlights on cars were covered with black paper with a small slit allowing a strip of light to dimly illuminate the way. Many accidents happened as cars and bicycles drove into the canals because no one was used to this practice. It was even dangerous to walk without a flashlight.

This situation did not prevent us from doing our daily work. We studied and hoped and believed that the war would be over soon. We thought that Germany had overextended itself by fighting on so many fronts. Little did we suspect what the next years would bring! Soon the Jews found that their daily lives were becoming more restricted; for example, Jews were not allowed to play sports in public places and clubs, so I had to give up my riding and fencing. It made me furious, but it was not the end of the world or so I thought, thus fooling myself into submission. Then in February of 1941, Jews were expelled from universities.

The Nazis defined a Jew as an individual who had four Jewish grandparents. This was probably because records in synagogues could be checked. Many of us were too scared to admit to being Jewish. I am quite sure that the Nazis rarely checked, but relied on the fears they induced to get the results they wanted. Rules restricting the level of education allowed to Jews were among the first instituted in Holland after the German occupation. Individuals with two Jewish grandparents (half Jews) were excluded from institutions of higher education but were allowed to enroll in trade schools or junior colleges. Full Jews however, were not even allowed that. My professors kindly allowed me to come into the college buildings at night. I studied bones, muscles and nerves in preparation for my exams. Working with a flashlight, I dismantled a skeleton, bone by bone. It was spooky but it was also exciting because I was defying the enemy. I thought that the war would end soon and I would be able to catch up with the other students; however, my professor became afraid that we would be caught and told me he could no longer let me come to his office at night. He was very sorry and assured me it was not personal. It was not an unusual reaction of non-Jews to remove themselves from the problems surrounding their Jewish friends out of fear of reprisal. There were rumors that this was happening in Germany. So my studies ended. I was already excluded from my sorority meetings because my sorority sisters were also afraid of consequences from the Nazis.

Kees, whose mother was a Jew and whose father was a minister, moved from Wageningen to Amsterdam to attend a technical school and came to visit me on the weekends. He lived with his brother, who was three years younger, not far from some of my relatives. Meanwhile, regulations concerning the Jewish population were the order of the day. Jews were barred now from using public transportation and personal means of transportation were confiscated. No reasons were ever given, just new rules that were published in newspapers and on posters attached to power poles all over town. My family became more frustrated and angry, as did many others, but still we did not realize the dangers of total isolation creeping up on us. Besides, there was still the widespread optimism that Germany would soon lose the war. That optimism gradually diminished.

A.

RIJKSUNIVERSITEIT TE UTRECHT.

STUDIEJAAR 1940—1941.

No. 813.

De RECTOR-MAGNIFICUS verklaart, dat

Mw. E. Dresden.

als STUDENT(E) is ingeschreven en mitsdien gedurende bovenvermeld studiejaar toegang heeft tot alle lessen der Rijksuniversiteiten, alsmede tot de daarbij behoorende inrichtingen en verzamelingen.

UTRECHT, den 23 SEP. 1940 194

[Handteekening van de(n) belanghebbende (ne varietur)].

Op aanvraag toonen.

Zonder bezit van deze kaart wordt de toegang geweigerd.

7888 - '40

Eline's registration certificate for medical school in Utrecht

I was unable to visit Kees in Amsterdam, so I never saw where he lived during that period. We wanted to get married, afraid that new regulations would separate us even more. Then we discovered that marriage between Jews and non-Jews was prohibited in order to maintain "purity of race." So another dream ended.

Despite all that had happened, the German authorities continued to assure us that there would be no alterations in our daily lives and that the Dutch government would remain intact. It was all too evident that this was not true. Little by little we had to adjust to changes and a passive acceptance came over us as we tried to resume our daily activities. Then the changes became more drastic. Everyone had to

DEPARTEMENT VAN OPVOEDING, WETENSCHAP EN CULTUURBESCHERMING.
No. 5206 Afd.H.O.
Betreffende:
Verordening no.28/1941.

Aan
Mejuffrouw E. Dresden,
Koningslaan 80,
Utrecht.

's-GRAVENHAGE, 8 October 1941.

In antwoord op Uw verzoekschrift van / Maart 1941 deel ik U mede, dat ik U geen toestemming kan verleenen om U voor het studiejaar 1941-1942 te laten inschrijven als student(e) in de faculteit der geneeskunde.

Voor den Secretaris-Generaal
van het Departement van Opvoeding, Wetenschap
en Cultuurbescherming,
Het Hoofd der Afdeeling,

Reinink

(Reinink).

Letter of refusal for enrollment in medical school:

To Miss E. Dresden
Konigslaan 80
Utrecht

s'Gravenhage, 8 October 1941

In answer to your request of March 1941, I hereby inform you that I cannot allow you to enroll for the college year 1941-42 in the medical school.

For the Secretary-General
of the Department of Education, Science and Culture.
Head of Faculty, Reinink

register at the courthouse to be given identification papers with photos and fingerprints. Food, gasoline, paper products, soap, and cooking gas were rationed. Again and again we adjusted and complied. It could no longer be denied: Jews were the target.

Not long after rationing was put into effect, the authorities decreed that Jews had to report to the courthouse with their identification cards. A big, fat, black letter "J" was stamped on both sides. Now the stage was set for the persecution to escalate. It was easy to seek out Jews wherever they dared to go. New restrictions were published and there was now a way to find out if the Jews were complying. Rules and regulations were announced every week, springing up like weeds overtaking a garden. It became difficult to move freely, to enter sports or entertainment facilities or government buildings. The Nazis timed the announcements of new restrictive policies in shrewd and insidious ways. As soon as citizens had recovered from the shock of the last insult, new rules were introduced. The flow of terrible events was relentless. Still, our passive acceptance remained.

My father was now the technical director of the large turbine factory in Utrecht. Of the four hundred people employed there, he was the only Jew. Early in 1941, a German officer came to conduct a safety inspection of the factory. When he asked if there was an air-raid alarm, my father said no. When he asked if there was a burglar alarm, my father again said no. When he asked if there was a guard dog, once again the answer was no. Aggravated, the man said, "If you have none of these things, then what do you have?" Father replied, "Fear." The officer responded, "Oh, humor. I like that very much, too!"

Soon, no Jew was allowed to be in a position of authority throughout all of Holland. Many people were fired from their jobs. Jewish professors were no longer allowed to teach. Jewish physicians could treat only Jews. Jews were barred from more and more public places. Curfews were imposed. Jews could shop only from three to six o'clock in the afternoons. And so it went.

On September 15, 1941, sums of one thousand guilders or more and all bonds and real estate owned by Jews were expropriated at the Lippmann Rosenthal Bank. My father came to the conclusion that he had to resign from his job, knowing that if he stayed, a special overseer would be appointed and he would lose his authority to manage the factory. The workers were upset over his leaving and many of them visited him at our home until even that was forbidden. The loss of income hit us hard. Father took some clandestine consulting jobs for large companies where he sat on the Boards of Directors, but because of the pervasive fears, these did not last long. Soon we had to start using our savings. Father had not had the chance to transfer his money to Switzerland for safety and the Nazis took possession of the stocks that he owned. Finances became even tighter, but we coped with the hardship and the restrictions in our lives by telling ourselves, "As long as we have our health, we can live this way. We will adjust. There are worse things in life." Worse, yes, beyond our wildest imaginations.

Daniel Dresden, Eline's Father

In the summer of 1940, looking forward to our college years and not yet affected by the regulations restricting the freedom of Jews, Kees and I went camping on the beach and visited my aunt, uncle, and cousins in The Hague. It was a wonderful time. We were still carefree and happy. I remember bringing my aunt a rabbit that she prepared for dinner.

In September, my fiancé moved into an apartment above a bakery with his friend, Harry. At five o'clock every morning the aroma of freshly baked rolls would engulf the bedroom which was just above the kitchen. I helped Kees and Harry make the place comfortable. The next weekend, Kees came to Utrecht and helped me fix up my room in a boarding house close to the medical school. Not yet fully aware of the coming events, we started our student years. We began to feel tormented by restrictions and anti-Semitic rules that constantly reminded us that we were outcasts.

In the midst of so many dangers and shattered hopes, Kees and I looked for mutual closeness and comfort, afraid to lose each other in those horrible times. In late 1941, I knew I was pregnant. My mother tried to convince me to have an abortion, even though it was illegal. She was quite agitated and predicted misery and tragedy for our future because of the war. Since the "Jewish problem" was not yet fully evident, I wonder now if she had an inkling of the Nazi's intentions. I was against abortion and did not want to have one. Above all, I loved Kees and our unborn child. Armed with the invincibility of youth, I was not afraid of hard times. My mother was a powerful person in my eyes, however, and rather than fight her, I agreed to find a doctor who would perform the abortion. I was convinced she would not be able to find a reputable doctor to do it, but I was wrong. She found a very fine doctor who was willing to help. He talked to me without my mother present and after I told him that Kees and I wanted the baby, he refused to do the abortion. For this I am still grateful. Although Kees and I were separated from each other and our child for many years, enduring much pain and hardship, we never regretted our decision.

In 1941, we were ordered to vacate our home because the German authorities wanted to use it. We were given twenty-four hours to empty the three-story house filled with the lifetime belongings of eight people. My family and friends worked hard. A faithful handyman removed the new carpet on the stairway and replaced it with the old carpet, which we had stored. The constant traffic on the stairs while he was working gave him a terrible headache. An armed guard posted by the front door constantly shouted, "*Schnell! Schnell!*" ("Hurry!"). It was evident that the Nazis enjoyed seeing frightened and submissive Jews.

We were not allowed to rent a moving van so we had to rely on friends with cars and loyal factory workers with trucks who came to help. We did not know where to take our possessions. They ended up in someone's attic or cellar. Many years afterward, we found some of our things, all wet and moldy, which we restored. But Father's publications and records of a lifetime of studies were lost when they were stacked on an uneven brick floor, fell over and got wet. Mother lost linen, silver table settings, photographs, paintings, sentimental knick-knacks, furniture, rugs, clothes, and personal memorabilia, everything except for a few clothes. As people were helping us, I heard comments such as, "I will take this," or "That would be nice at my house." And always the amused guards at the door, taking pleasure in our distress.

The house at Konigslaan 80 in Utrecht that had to be vacated in twenty-four hours.

Soon, my pregnancy was advanced enough to be evident. The *Schutzstaffel* (the "S.S." or German Guard Corps) made comments about Jews having more Jews, thus providing more to kill. Fortunately, I was strong and able to work hard. After a long sleepless night, the eleven-room house was empty. An *Obersturmführer* (high-ranking officer) conducted the inspection and became infuriated when he saw the outlines on the wallpaper where the pictures had been and dents in the hardwood floor where the piano used to sit. He decided that the German personnel should be comfortable and ordered that everything be returned within twenty-four hours. We did not even know where most of our belongings were but we tried to bring everything back, including the silverware and pictures. Then, it was all gradually confiscated. I think it is ironic that we were given receipts for many objects. I still have the receipt for my father's bicycle, noting that the bell did not work and the tires were worn.

GEMEENTE UTRECHT C 59

INLEVERING: RIJWIELEN VAN JODEN
EINNAHME: FAHRRÄDER VON JUDEN

Empfangen von :
Ontvangen van :
Name
Naam Dresden
Vorname
Voornaam Daniël
Wohnhaft (Strasse)
Woonplaats (straat) Adr. v. Ostadelaan No 13
ein Fahrrad / een rijwiel { Kinder / Damen / Herren } durchstreichen was nicht angebracht ist / doorstrepen wat niet toepasselijk is
ein Zweirad
een Tandem
Gestellnummer
Nummer 3830
Fabrikmarke
Merk ———
Bereifung (mit/ohne)
Banden (met of zonder) met banden
Qualität der Bereifung / Toestand van de banden { ~~gut~~ / ~~mittel~~ / schlecht } durchstreichen was nicht angebracht ist / doorstrepen wat niet toepasselijk is
Bemerkungen betr. fehlende Teile :
(ohne Lampe – ohne Bremse) bel ontbreekt
Aanteekening betreffende ontbrekende onderdeelen :
(zonder lamp – zonder rem)

Utrecht, 29 Juni 1942.

Der Oberbürgermeister von Utrecht,
im Auftrag (namens hem)

Receipt for the bicycle confiscated by the Nazis noting condition of the tires and missing bell.

One of the few items to survive the Nazis' grand-scale thievery was a liquid soap dispenser that my father had brought from Norway the previous year. It was quite a novelty at the time and Mother was very fond of it. It was made of two hollow clear glass hemispheres held together by a horizontal metal strip, forming an orb. It was suspended in a holder by a bracket attached to the metal strip, enabling it to tilt. Liquid soap would then come out of a hole in the top hemisphere. I decided to save this elegant object and my means of doing so was a flowing, light green wool coat, with round fake tiger-fur pockets that I wore during my pregnancy. Because of its wide drape I could easily hide the soap dispenser underneath and smuggle it past the guard. What a triumph this was! It was my first taste of active resistance and the sense of power was euphoric and worth the risk. In the following years I was able to save or steal many other things. This was an extremely dangerous practice for which I could have paid with my life, but it served to help me retain some feeling of control and that made me stronger and better able to survive.

After we were made to return everything to our former home, we spent two nights at the house of Jewish friends. We were not allowed to stay in any non-Jewish home. We rented a house close to our own and bought and borrowed furniture, eating utensils and pots and pans, thinking that we could live a normal life again, not anticipating the transient course our lives were to take. Looking back on those times I realize how we lived in an illusion fed by wishful fantasy, but the desire for something familiar and normal was compelling. We should have known better, but we really did not recognize the monstrous qualities of our persecutors. We should have known ... but how?

When the time came to deliver my baby, I walked three-quarters of a kilometer to the hospital because I was not allowed to take public transportation or a taxi and my bicycle had been confiscated. Daniel Adrianus (nicknamed "Daantje" and pronounced "Dahnt-ya") was born on April 28, 1942. He came into the world with the sounds of the German "Flag" (*flugzeugabwehgeschütz*: anti-aircraft cannons). We lived beneath the flight pattern of the Allied bombers and there was a steady stream of airplanes all night. The sky lit up with the white puffs of exploding ammunition while I cried. It was a difficult birth, but Kees was allowed in the delivery room to comfort me. Daantje weighed a healthy eight and a half pounds. I stayed in the hospital for ten days. A notary public legalized the surname, Hoekstra, for Daniel because Kees and I were prohibited from marrying.

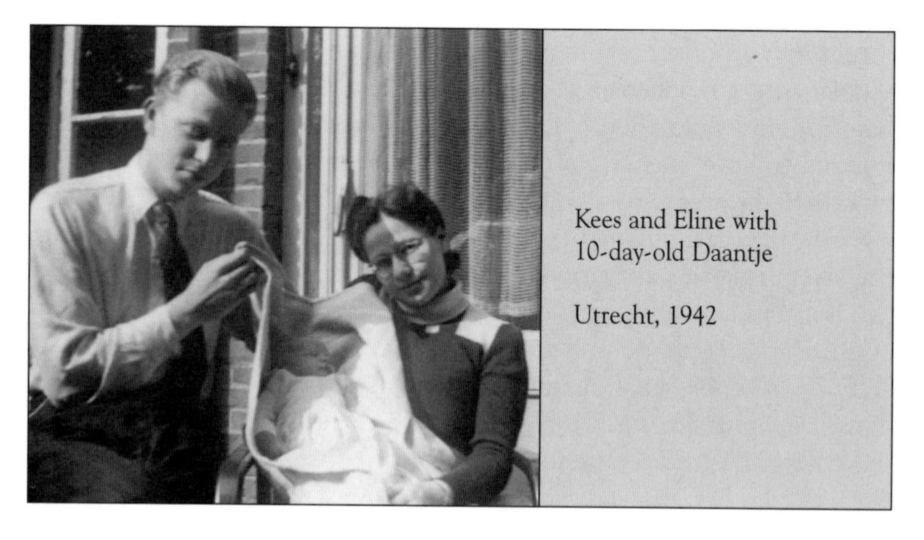

Kees and Eline with 10-day-old Daantje

Utrecht, 1942

On the first of May, two days after I gave birth, the authorities ordered all Jews to wear the yellow Star of David insignia in public. My mother bought the stars for me while I was in the hospital. She sewed one on my coat, as this had to be done before I was allowed to leave the hospital. I actually had pride in the symbol, not knowing the terrible hardship that was in store for those of us wearing it. I drew a lot of attention wearing the yellow brand as I walked home from the hospital, stopping to rest several times on my suitcase.

As time went by we became increasingly removed from the familiarity of our daily lives. We could neither visit nor receive non-Jews in our house; however, two loyal non-Jewish friends did visit us one night. Jews as well as their friends risked grave consequences for violating rules. They were taken to the offices of the German police and were often detained indefinitely. This happened to one of our friends and yet some faithful ones did not abandon us. We entertained ourselves by working on a jigsaw puzzle. (Our puzzles had been assembled so many times that we turned them face down to increase the challenge). We also read so much that we had to share books by tearing them down the middle and exchanging the halves with each other.

One night the doorbell suddenly rang. This was followed by a loud banging and the voices of the police shouting at us to open up. My father turned pale and went to the door as the knocking continued. It was the police. They liked to terrorize people and they succeeded with me. I could hardly breathe as I looked for a place to hide. In my state of panic I hid behind a curtain, not thinking of the bulge I made behind it. Beside myself with fear, I tried to listen to what was going on. The police told us that there were two bicycles outside leaning against the wall of the house and that they could easily be stolen. We thanked them and sighed with relief after they left. It took the rest of the night for us to calm down. Talking about what might have been, we went back to our puzzle and counted our blessings. We had survived another night.

* * * * * *

My maternal grandfather, Eduard Strelitskie, was a short man with a whimsical face, full of energy, dreams and love of life. He always made jokes and walked with a spring in his step. He aspired to be an artist but followed his father's directive and worked as a diamond cutter instead. After he retired, he designed and painted large movie banners that hung outside theaters, depicting scenes from coming attractions, thus partially fulfilling his dream. He employed two young men as helpers and they worked in the front room of my grandparents' home. My grandmother always admired her husband and tolerated a perpetually dirty hallway with people coming and going all day and sometimes during the night when there was a rush order.

Grandmother Strelitskie (born Celine Baggers) was an attractive, petite woman who loved music and played piano with crooked arthritic fingers well into her seventies. She took pride in the fact that she could speak some French. She had learned the language when she was fourteen years old and lived with an aunt in Paris during the World's Fair when the Eiffel Tower was built. At that time it was not unusual for men with sharp knives to scout around in crowds looking to cut off the long hair of young girls to sell to a wig maker. Stealing it was quick and painless. Sometimes the girl did not even notice her hair was cut off just below hat level until she arrived home. While at the fair, this happened to my grandmother. Despite that, the time she spent in Paris was the highlight of her teenage years.

Grandmother Strelitskie was a born actress and often would imitate people, sometimes right in front of them. Once she mimicked a store

Marcel Strelitskie, Eline's uncle, who was a cabaret performer.

1938

clerk with a speech impediment and embarrassed my grandfather so much that he walked out. She would imitate odd expressions she saw on the faces of people on the trolley or she would ape the limp of a person walking in front of her. When I was a child I thought this was funny, but of course it was impolite. She took me to Tarzan movies and had as much fun as I did. Grandfather lovingly served her breakfast in bed each morning from the first day of their marriage. She worked hard in the household, often late into the night, but she hated to get up early and so he pampered her in this way. Breakfast was always a fried egg, two pieces of toast with jam and a mug of strong hot coffee. I got the same and we giggled together as we planned the day.

I had such fun with them! Grandfather liked to tease. I remember traveling with him to Utrecht as he carried two large suitcases. A young man offered to help him. Grandfather, feigning annoyance, said, "What's the matter? You think I don't carry them right?" But then he quickly thanked the man.

My grandparents had four children. David was the oldest, followed by Marcel, my mother, Mietje, and Eduard ("Eddie") who came eighteen years later. My father was a friend of David, a smart and friendly personality, but a rift developed in their friendship when David took up with a promiscuous woman. My father cautioned him that she was trouble and could have a venereal disease but David would not believe him. He eventually broke off with her, married another woman and had children. It was discovered later that he had contracted syphilis and so he took the cure of that time, which was the induction of malaria to cause high fever. Although it did cure him, the fever left him with severe brain damage. He became vegetative and flat and his physical strength declined. He was put in an asylum by his wife but was retrieved by his father who brought him home. His life was reduced to stuffing and sealing envelopes. I never found out when or to which internment camp he was taken. There was a rumor that he was taken to Belgium and then to Dachau.

Marcel became a cabaret artist who was well known in Holland, Belgium and France. Between contracts he lived with his parents. I remember a grand piano in his room and lots of memorabilia from his performances. He was detained in the latter part of 1941, and was taken to Amersfoort, a city south of Utrecht. Amersfoort was also the name of one of the more brutal transition camps, as we later found out from escapees and residents of that city. It received not only Jews, but also individuals accused of crimes. We hoped that as an entertainer there was a chance that he would be spared harsh treatment, but we never heard from him again. My grandparents had to endure the anguish of not knowing what happened to their sons. At that time none of us knew that Jews were being murdered. Many years later, I found the names of my uncles in the death books in Yad Vashem, the Holocaust Memorial in Israel. Marcel was killed in Auschwitz on the fifth of November, 1942.

The youngest son, Eddie, married a non-Jewish woman and they had three children before and during the war. Being in a mixed marriage with children allowed him exemption from transport. He survived, became well known for his paintings and taught at the Art Academy in The Hague for many years. After the war, his family was enriched with three more children.

Escaping the treatment that other Jews suffered did not give my uncle much peace of mind because it was known that some zealous Nazis would detain individuals in mixed marriages, saying they would investigate the situation later. Often the investigation would not occur, but the detainee would disappear forever. For a while, Eddie avoided danger by keeping a low profile but as time went by and the situation grew more serious, he went into hiding in the home of our faithful Plie.

My mother's parents were originally from Amsterdam as were my father's. My parents lived for a time in The Hague. When my mother's father retired, her parents decided to move there to be close to their only grandchildren – my siblings and me. Many years later, we moved to Utrecht, an hour away from The Hague by train. Grandfather's movie banner business kept him in The Hague and I visited them often. When the German forces occupied The Netherlands, my parents worried about my grandparents but they assured us they would be all right. Eighteen months after the occupation, the Nazis rounded up the older Jews living in larger cities and moved them to Amsterdam. They were not allowed to take their belongings other than clothes and a few personal effects. We were fortunate enough to get permission for my grandparents to stay with us in Utrecht "until further notice." They arrived in March 1942, when I was eight months pregnant. They were delighted to be with us and eagerly anticipated the birth of their first great-grandchild. I still fondly remember their intense excitement when I went to the hospital. When I came home with my newborn son, my seventy-five year old grandfather serenaded us on his violin while standing on a homemade podium.

One day in July, some good friends warned us that the S.S. was rounding up elderly people in order to transport them to Amsterdam. There was no time to find a hiding place but we had to do something, so we decided to stage a scene. We knew that the Nazis did not like sick people, especially if they had contagious diseases, so my mother put on her nurse's uniform and gathered up ether, syringes and Lysol to set the stage. My grandparents came from a family of actors and knew how to put on a show. They both played their parts as invalids very convincingly. I remember them lying in their bed, the only piece of furniture that they were allowed to bring with them from The Hague. It was made of black iron with gold-colored balls on top of each post. Grandmother had long, wavy white hair and false teeth. She removed her teeth, powdered her face to a pale white, shook her hair loose and greased it up with petroleum jelly to appear sweaty and feverish. She lay back on her pillow and moaned. Grandfather had a hernia, was bald and toothless. He didn't believe in false teeth, saying, "If God meant me to have teeth he wouldn't have taken them away!" We hooked the elastic bandage for his hernia on the bedpost as he tilted his head onto the pillow and moaned. The weather was hot and humid and the odor was nauseating. The set was complete.

I climbed a tree in the backyard, lucky to be pregnant no longer. My baby was not in the house that day because there had been rumors of raids. In about an hour, the black-booted, green-uniformed thugs came down the street to our house. They banged on the door and pressed on the bell, their usual practice designed to heighten the fear of the occupants. There were two S.S. men and a Dutch collaborator with the *Nationale Socialistische Bewegung* (the "N.S.B." or National Socialistic Movement, an organization of Nazi collaborators).

My mother scurried around with medicine as my grandparents groaned. When the German police officers asked what was wrong, we told them that a doctor had diagnosed dysentery. It worked. The men left quickly. I scrambled out of the tree and we went in the bedroom where we laughed until the tears ran. The officers came back. We replayed the scene and they left again. Although we were relieved we did not dare to celebrate yet. We were happy yet apprehensive at the same time, knowing that danger was still present. The ruse gave my grandparents a few weeks of respite and it was well worth the effort.

Finally, my grandparents were forced to obey the orders to move to Amsterdam and they were put on a transport. They had to leave behind the bed that they had shared for fifty years, the bed on which my grandmother had delivered her children. They also left behind their personal possessions: a hairbrush, family photographs, shaving tools, and Grandfather's inscribed ivory cigarette holder that was his pride and joy. They were allowed to take only a few clothes. They were placed in a facility for elderly invalids who had been rounded up from all over the country. My father was able to visit them in Amsterdam a few times, using his special permit that allowed him to travel by train for Jewish affairs. After a couple of weeks, they were herded into the Jewish Theater with other older people to await transport. None of us knew their destination or their future. They were put in cattle cars on a train, each holding about seventy people. Many detainees pushed postcards

Celine Strelitskie

Eduard Strelitskie

between the wood slats, hoping someone would pick them up and mail them. We received such a postcard that my grandparents had thrown from the train, mailed by a compassionate stranger. They wrote that they would be lonely for us, but that they would be all right and would make themselves useful. Grandmother was good at darning socks and Grandfather was an excellent potato peeler. Surely the authorities would appreciate these skills. Surely soldiers always ate potatoes and wore socks. We didn't believe they would survive harsh treatment; we could only hope that they would not suffer long. It was years later that we discovered the train took them to Auschwitz.

* * * * * *

On May 1, 1942, the Nazi regime declared that all Jews had to wear the yellow Star of David on the left side of their chests at all times, except when in their own homes. Years later, I learned that the color yellow was chosen for the stars because historically, ships carrying pestilence had to fly a yellow flag and were not allowed to dock in harbors. Hitler often referred to Jews as "the pests of society."

When housewives went outside to meet the baker or vegetable vendor and talk with neighbors, they had to remember to wear the star. Jews certainly stood out at these gatherings. We were made to buy the stars from a dry goods store, paying for them with the textile "points" rationed for us to buy clothes. The form of the star was printed on a square of yellow cotton cloth. We had to cut it out and sew it on to a piece of backing to give it enough body to hold its form. They were expensive. We had three apiece. Since it was required that they be sewn onto our clothing, we came up with the idea of sewing them on short vests that we called *bolero*. We could then put them on over whatever we were wearing. For safety, we wore them indoors as well. We knew that if a person in possession of an I.D. card with the designation "J" was ever caught without the star, they risked never returning home. The majority of Jews obeyed the star rule out of fear of non-compliance. We also thought it united us and showed our solidarity and pride in being Jewish. As I look back on events, I am struck with the naiveté of this thinking because we had every reason to be frightened. I now think that what courage we had should have been saved for other situations.

My sister had a good Jewish friend, Lotti Frijda, who decided not to wear the star. The S.S. stopped her on the street, ordered her off of her bicycle and demanded to see her identification, which was stamped with the letter "J." Bystanders watched as she was taken away to the police station. She probably was told that her case would be "investigated," as this was the way it often worked, but the investigation never happened. She was taken to the internment camp, Westerbork, transported somewhere "east" and we never heard from her again. She was twenty-two years old.

This was not an uncommon occurrence. I knew several people who suffered the same fate. If the S.S. thought a person looked Jewish, they were categorized as such, whether it was true or not. The S.S. was trained by the Nazis to recognize Jews by caricature drawings of ugly men and women with hook noses, curly hair and brown eyes.

When I went to Israel in 1992, I searched in the death books in the library at the memorial museum, Yad Vashem, for the name of Lotti Frijda. I did not find it. If time had allowed, I am sure I would have found it either in the records at Dachau or Mauthausen or perhaps another camp. The records are scrupulously complete. The German record-keepers were very systematic and precise.

In June 1942, we were starting to fully realize the effect of the war on our daily lives, although we had escaped actual warfare as there was no fighting in Holland after our capitulation. When the United States entered into the war, there were air attacks on Germany, especially in the area of Hamburg, and Bremen, so Holland was in the flight pattern. The sirens, warning of Allied bombers overhead, sounded several times a day and increased in frequency at night making sleep difficult and leaving us exhausted. In areas where houses were hit, one could see a stairway and sometimes a chimney still standing. There were no bomb shelters because Holland had never anticipated the need; however, I believe there were some built after the occupation in the larger cities. As Jews were subject to curfew, we would not have been able to use them anyway.

There was no comfort to be had for my little baby, Daantje. My mother and I spent many long nighttime hours in the safest spots in the house, under the staircase or in the bathroom. We put Daantje's bassinet in those places and hoped for the best. The darkness caused by the blackened windows heightened the sinister atmosphere and sense of hardship and I was so afraid for my baby. But we were lucky and never suffered a "hit" or flying debris. My mother would sit with me through the night and we were happy when morning came and the black curtains could be removed. Relieved at having survived one more night, we would pretend that life was normal and make breakfast. But that pretense became harder to maintain as the threat of being rousted from our home grew greater. This was even worse than the fear triggered by the air raids.

Raids on Jews began in Amsterdam where most of them lived. Later more raids were carried out in Utrecht, Rotterdam, The Hague, and other larger cities. At first they occurred only at night, then during the day as well. Terrorist acts were rampant as the Jews were driven into ghettos. If resistance was encountered, the authorities used the quickest and most effective deterrent, which is the punishment and torture of loved ones. If a man protested, his wife was kicked or shot. If the wife cried, the terrified children were dragged out and transported away.

We knew that the raids were coming to our city and that most of them were happening at night. To try to ensure Daantje's safety, I developed a routine. Each afternoon I took him outside in his baby carriage, packed with diapers and bottles of breast milk that I had pumped. Three blocks from home I would meet up with my good friend, Corrie, a faithful housekeeper who had worked for us for many years and lived nearby. In order not to arouse notice, we talked for awhile. Then she left with the baby in his carriage and I walked home. In the morning we reversed the procedure.

Eline with her baby, Daantje

Utrecht, 1942

During the day we tried to have the semblance of a normal life with Daantje by playing with him, bathing him, changing his diapers and nursing him. But there was always tension and fear. We decided that if the Nazis came we would tell them that Daantje was the son of a visitor who was Jewish but married to a non-Jew. He had blonde hair and blue eyes and, of course, he could not say his name and reveal the deception.

One afternoon, the doorbell rang. I was home with a young woman named Stien who was spending time at our house for the purpose of posing as Daantje's mother. At this time it was not yet forbidden for Jews to have non-Jewish visitors. The urgency of the bell's clapper ringing non-stop was a surefire clue that it was either the S.S. or a Dutch collaborator. I opened the peep window and asked what they wanted. An S.S. man asked for me by name. I said, "I'll see if she's home." I quickly instructed Stien on how to act, then I went back to the door to tell the officers I would check upstairs. They rang the bell again. I told them I could not find her and would check the basement. I was trying to buy time so I could think of what to do. It was obvious they didn't believe me. I was also worried that my mother would return home and be caught with the contraband food coupons she had gone out to get. I ran into the backyard and tried to climb a tall wood fence. At the top, I came face to face with the S.S. man. He said, "You must have a guilty conscience since you are trying to escape." He shoved me to the ground with a gun between my shoulder blades. The black-booted officers grinned as they lowered the gun. They went through the house, taking items they liked, including an alarm clock. (This unauthorized stealing was actually unusual behavior for the S.S.) They asked me if I were the one they sought. When I said that I was, they grinned and replied, "We just wanted to have a little fun and scare you!" Then they left. My mother arrived five minutes later. My whole body trembled uncontrollably and I was so shaken that I could not produce breast milk for Daantje. I regained control very slowly. The men had apparently believed that Daantje was Stien's child.

It became clear that Daantje would have to be hidden. Arrangements had been made with Nel Vermey and her mother, Grandmother "Oma" Dinger, affluent non-Jewish friends of my father. I was not informed of their names in order to protect them, my child and myself. They lived in a large, elegant house in s'Graveland in the countryside, with greenhouses and chickens on the property. It was important that they had money, enabling them to buy food on the black market during this time of strict rationing. But most important of all, they were willing to take the risk to save Daantje. What a risk it was indeed! If they had been discovered, they would have met the same fate as the Jews. They concocted an explanation for Daantje's presence: his mother had been killed by stray allied bombs and his father was not able to take care of him. Kees would be able to visit him at the "war home" for as a half-Jew, he was still allowed to travel. I packed his suitcase with diapers, sweaters and other necessities, and then nursed him for the last time. He fed quickly and seemed to swallow a lot of air.

Daantje with the Vermey family, who cared for him during the war.

s'Graveland, 1943

He cried as he lay on the bed next to the suitcase. I thought he was having gas pains and did not stop packing to burp him because of the urgency I felt. I thought my anxiety was affecting him. He cried louder and louder as I tried to close the lid of the suitcase. I wanted him to stop but it got worse and worse. The suitcase was so full I could not close it, so I sat on it. Suddenly, I realized that his little finger was caught under the lid! He was not injured because his finger was still so small and pliable, but my feelings of guilt, hysteria and nausea are vivid to this day.

I took Daantje on our routine walk down the block where we again met up with Corrie. She kept him at her house for several days and then took him to his protectors. It was August 13, 1942. He was three and a half months old.

*   *   *   *   *   *

The German authorities compiled many lists that categorized Jewish individuals according to particular criteria. There was a "Diamond" list, a "Swiss" list, an "Intellectuals" list, a "Baptized Jews" list, and so on. It seemed that the purpose of these lists was to perpetuate the illusion that one could postpone or be spared from the dreadful fate that befell those not on such a list. We did not put faith in the power of a list to save us; in fact, we suspected that certain ones such as the Diamond or Swiss lists were a means to extract wealth from Jews hoping to buy their way out of dangerous circumstances. But we decided to try to get on a list just in case it had some beneficial effect. The Diamond list was not accessible to us since we were not in the jewelry business and had no way to obtain gems. My father had done some technical work for Palestine (now Israel), some years before the war, and thinking it might be a way to get out of the hands of the Nazis, we tried to get on the Palestine list. In fact, while we were initially detained at our first imprisonment site, we received a note from the International Red Cross, dated June 25, 1943, stating that we had been granted a certificate of immigration to Palestine. But there was no way to get there.

Nel Vermey, Daanjte's "War Mother," and Daantje, age one

s'Graveland, 1943

My father, his parents, and our family qualified to get on the Intellectuals list and did, but my mother's parents did not. We were led to believe that by being categorized as such, we would not be sent "east" and could stay where we lived. We were elated and relieved, yet skeptical. We had seen these lists "*platzt*" (burst like a balloon)

K 360

HET NEDERLANDSCHE ROODE KRUIS
AFDEELING AMSTERDAM

AMSTERDAM Z., Nic. Maesstraat 55
Tel. 24200. Postgiro 280400

25 Juni 1943

Den Hooggeleerden Heer Prof.Dresden.
Barneveld.

Het Internationale Roode Kruis te Genève verzoekt ons U mede te deelen, dat U en Uwe familie een immigratiecertificaat voor toegang in Palestina hebben ontvangen voor de tweede veteranenlijst.

Uebersetzung:
Das Internationale Rote Kreuz in Genf hat uns gebeten Ihnen mit zuteilen, dass für Sie und Ihre Familie ein Zertificat zur Einwanderung nach Palästina auf der zweiten Veteranenliste ausgestellt worden ist.

Namens den Secretaris van het Afdeelingsbestuur

Bestuurslid

DUTCH RED CROSS
AMSTERDAM DIVISION

To the Erudite Professor Dresden
Barneveld

25 June 1943

The International Red Cross in Geneva asked us to notify you that you and your family have received an immigration certificate for entry into Palestine for the second veteran's list.

(same text in German)

In the name of the Secretary of the Division Board

overnight, rendering worthless the promise of protection. All the lists contained this disclaimer clause *bis auf weiters* ("until further notice"), giving the Nazis yet another means to torment their prey. We later learned that the Intellectuals list and the Baptized Jews list may indeed have had real value and perhaps helped to save our lives.

Most of the individuals on the Intellectuals list found themselves transferred to Theresienstadt (Terezin) in Czechoslovakia, a small city that had been turned into a ghetto. Even though life was quite harsh there, about eighty percent of the people who stayed there survived. Many, however, were transported from there to other camps. The construction of the gas chambers in Theresienstadt had been started, but was never completed.

The order came for all Jews to turn in their wedding rings and other valuables. We had complied with similar confiscation orders. We had already handed over our primary mode of transportation, our bicycles, for which we were given detailed receipts, instilling the act with a sense of legitimacy that was totally bogus. Soon after that we had to turn in our radios (which were our source of information about the war) and our cameras (which had enabled us to document our family history), and many other precious items. The timing of these orders, like the issuance of the other restrictions, was shrewdly planned. Just as we got accustomed to the loss of certain items and were lulled into a state of sad acceptance, the next order came. This method of gradual deprivation was designed to make us realize that we could do without material objects and that our highest priority was life itself, however restricted and harsh it was made to be.

A poor handyman who worked for us for many years (the same one who changed the carpet on our stairway) offered to keep my parents' wedding rings and my rings for us. Despite his poverty and having nine children to support, he never sold our valuables and returned them to us after the war. We heard that he died of tuberculosis.

* * * * * *

In August 1942, I had Daantje safely placed. It was time for me to go. I was torn about this decision. I was afraid to go, yet afraid to stay. Two kind women that my father knew were willing to take me in. It was a remarkably courageous act because of the penalties for harboring Jews. The woman, whose name I can't remember, and her housekeeper lived in a comfortable third-floor apartment that was a ten-minute walk from our house. She worked in the daytime while the housekeeper did the shopping, cleaning and household management. Shopping took a long time because of rationing and the long lines at each store. The women had to be careful about how much food they purchased in order to avoid suspicion. Perhaps the milkman or the baker would notice if a little extra milk or another loaf of bread was bought, so they bought supplies illegally, but carefully, going to shops they did not usually patronize.

I had to be very careful about making noise such as flushing the toilet, running the faucet or closing a door so that other residents in the building would not hear me. I had to walk softly and avoid going near windows where I would easily have been seen by passers-by in the narrow street. Many people in the neighborhood knew me and I had to avoid being reported. To keep busy I read, studied and disentangled the knots from yarn. This latter activity was quiet and I made little wool animals for Daantje to help me feel connected to him. I became more frightened each day. I stopped reading for fear that I would fall asleep and drop the book and make a noise. When the phone rang, I jumped; when the doorbell rang I was scared. One day as I was there alone, the phone and the doorbell rang at the same time. I could feel my heart pound in my throat and I couldn't breathe. Clammy with sweat, I couldn't move my limbs. Panicked, I hid under the couch.

When the housekeeper came home I told her I could not live this way. Maybe I had a better chance in a "labor" camp where we thought Jews were sent. She understood and so after two weeks, I went back home.

In looking back today, I believe that I might have been better able to cope in a death camp than in hiding as the extreme measures of a clandestine life were too hellish for me to bear. Forced to be passive, I became a tight bundle of nerves, scared all the time. Had I been caught I would have been transported straight to a death camp anyway. It was the fate of those who hid.

In the spring of 1942, Kees was twenty years old. In the dark hours of early morning, he was picked up in Amsterdam with hundreds of other young men, in retaliation for the murder of General Seyffert, a high-ranking Nazi official. Not all were Jewish, but they were targeted for the purpose of general terrorism. We received word of this from Kees' younger brother, Johan, who lived with him in Amsterdam. The S.S. had come around five o'clock in the morning and had taken Kees away. I can still hear my own anguished cries upon hearing the news.

Kees was taken to Vught in central Holland, along with the other young men. It was known to be a particularly brutal camp that practiced a torture resulting in many quick deaths. My intense fear and hatred of the Nazis escalated even more. It was ironic that the one "half-Jew" in our family was detained before the rest of us. It was even more ironic that the German authorities were concerned about their public image in Holland during this time. Due to the united efforts of the Dutch churches, who put pressure on the authorities to institute some acts of compassion, several men were released from the camp. Luckily, Kees was one of them. He was seriously ill with the "blue measles," a highly virulent and contagious disease, when he came to our house in Utrecht. He was sick for three weeks. By then I had contracted the same disease. Kees eventually went back to Amsterdam to go to school where he lived again with his younger brother who had not been taken away. All this turned out to be something of a blessing because the Nazi "super race" was afraid of communicable diseases. We were quarantined, giving my family a six-week delay from being transported to our first internment camp, *Kasteel de Schaffelaar,* in Barneveld.

Chapter 3

INTERNMENT

On April 21, 1943, two S.S. officers came to our house. They ordered us to be ready in half an hour to board a bus that was to take us to the castle De Schaffelaar in Barneveld, a city thirty kilometers east of Utrecht. Although the castle had not been inhabited for years and was so dilapidated that the tower was ready to fall down, it was used to house imprisoned Jews. Our being on the Intellectuals list probably led us to this "elite" camp. The population of De Schaffelaar consisted of approximately four hundred "intellectuals." I went there with my parents and oldest brother, Daniel. (The younger of the two brothers, Tony, had moved to the United States in 1939. My sister went into hiding, working as an x-ray technician for the older brother of her inital saviour, Dr. Arendsen Hein.) We were told we would not be transported elsewhere – a political gesture by the Nazis to the remnant of the Dutch government – but on the official documents there was always the qualifying phrase, "until further notice," which we learned to recognize as a sinister foreboding.

In the city was a place called "De Biezen" where about the same number of Jews were held captive. This was the group of baptized Protestant and Catholic Jews. These internment locations were in use for less than a half year and are not widely known, but they are noted in the *Atlas of the Holocaust*.

The Tudor-style castle was built in 1852. The hallways had high ceilings that bounced back hollow echoes. There was no plumbing in the upstairs areas. The rooms were as big as meeting halls and were partitioned off with pieces of plywood. There were no toilets for the four hundred people housed there. Outhouses were constructed to accommodate the needs of the many who had come from comfortably heated homes with bathrooms. The precarious tower was converted to accommodate about eight hundred people. Separate barracks were constructed on the grounds to serve as eating areas and to function as hospital quarters for the sick. Many of the elderly suffered from heart

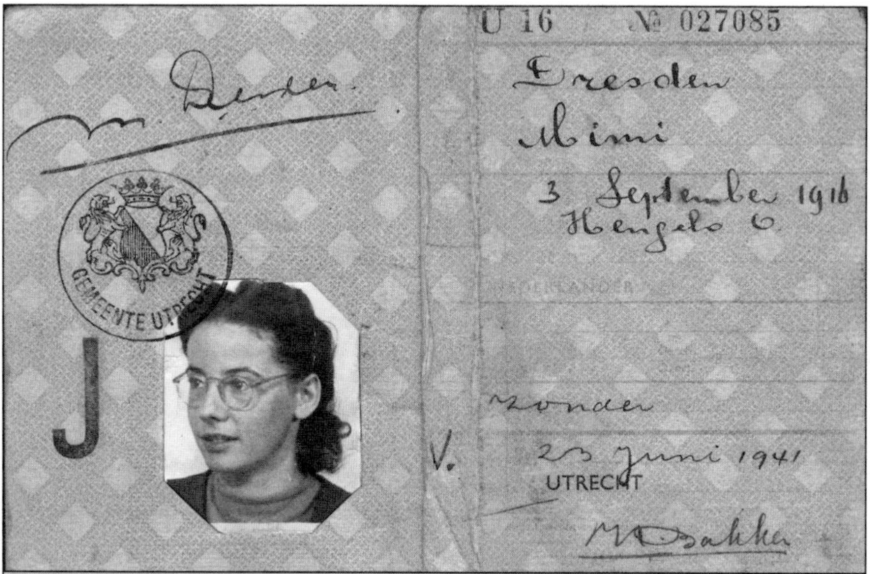

German-issued identification card for Mimi Dresden.

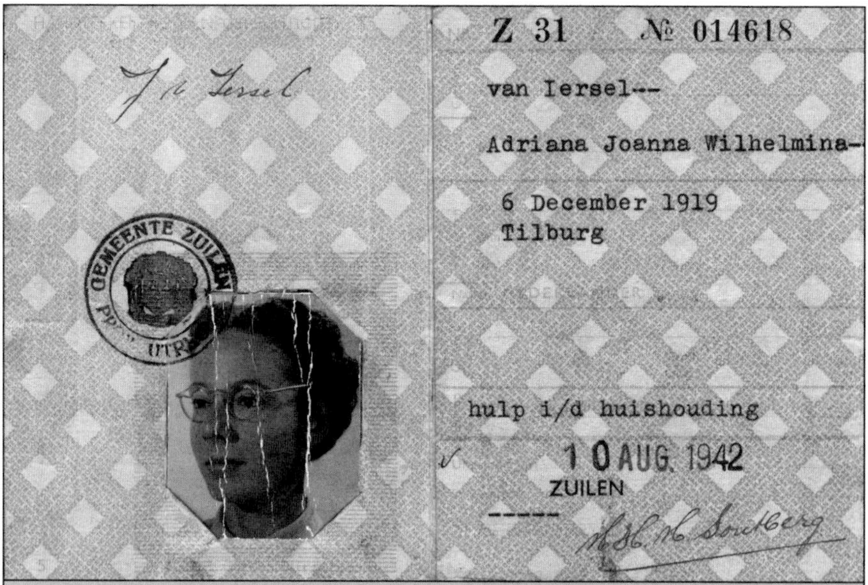

Mimi Dresden's fake identification card. Note the missing "J" for "Jew".

problems, exhaustion, arthritis and general malaise. Tension and apprehension were widespread. Adjusting to the living conditions was not the most difficult thing for me; the lack of privacy was.

As many as three families were housed in each of the small rooms in the upper level of the main castle. My family stayed in the barracks. The cramped nature of the quarters was intensified by the chaos of crying babies. Everyone worried about relatives who could not join this "privileged" group. Many heated arguments occurred among this congregation of frightened Jews who had been robbed of their dignity and their futures and were at the mercy of a handful of hostile, hateful Nazi guards.

German armband printed with the words "Street Permit" that allowed the wearer to be on the streets after curfew. This one came into the possession of Eline's sister, Mies, while in a convent during the war.

Someone munching on a crisp cracker could drive another into a rage. Most people suffered from intestinal problems, fouling the air and we had to constantly fight disgust, nausea and irritation. We felt demeaned by not being able to attend to matters of personal hygiene, yet we had to bring up compassion and tolerance, if only to save our own sanity.

Life at the castle had a surrealistic quality. The building, though old, was beautiful and displayed remnants of a bygone luxurious life; yet we felt threatened as we waited for worse things to happen to us. We were allowed to take walks on the fenced grounds, however, and could receive visitors and packages. I was even granted a travel permit to see my doctor in Utrecht once a month. Kees met me at the train station in Utrecht and we would go together to Plie's house. He also visited me at De Schaffelaar where we walked in the wooded area and lay in each other's arms in the autumn leaves, hoping to regain the life that had slipped away. Kees was eventually sent to a labor camp in Germany and so the visits stopped.

There were many sick people in this camp, as resistance to illness was low. It was an ideal breeding ground for desperation and disease including scarlet fever, diphtheria, measles, strep infections and, always, dysentery. I contracted the dreaded scarlet fever as well as diphtheria and suffered middle-ear infections that damaged my hearing. I stayed in the sleeping quarters in an upper bunk for days, soaking the filthy sheets with profuse sweating or shivering constantly with no blankets. I vomited and was delirious. My parents came to see me often. A doctor came twice a day to put cold compresses on my forehead and tried to comfort me. There were many excellent doctors at the castle, but they felt helpless and lost, as there was no medicine. My fever finally broke, but I continued to be apprehensive because it was possible that I had sustained damage to my heart. After several weeks I got up, weak and wobbly. I felt as though I were living a horrible nightmare. Had I been in any other internment camp I probably would not have survived.

One beautiful afternoon, September 28, 1943 (the Jewish New Year), we were suddenly surrounded by S.S. guards, N.S.B. officers (the Nazi party in Holland), and the Green Police (an elite Nazi corps that used Doberman Pinschers and German Shepherd dogs.) The entire population of captives at Castle De Schaffelaar was herded to the train depot and onto a train with several compartments. We were each allowed to take one bag with us; my brother, Daniel, carried an attaché case. Several individuals tried to escape; only a few were successful. Most of us boarded the train without resistance. Each compartment had its own door and held about eight individuals. I was with my parents, my brother and other unrelated people. We felt dazed as the train began to move. The familiar huffing and puffing of the steam engine that had always seemed so romantic to me was now foreboding and frightening.

No one knew where we were being taken or why. We were filled with despair and a sense of doom. As I recall this event, I am struck by how hope and the desire to survive enabled us to withstand yet another injury, another injustice, another insult – always a little more.

Castle "De Schaffelaar" as it is today.

(photo by Faith Yang)

We left Barneveld in the early afternoon. We could tell by the direction of the setting sun that we were traveling north. The train moved slowly. Daniel was unusually quiet and seemed immersed in his thoughts. At dusk, we arrived at Hooghalen where the train had to switch tracks. As it slowed almost to a halt, Daniel opened the compartment door and quietly jumped out. My mother wanted to scream, but my father covered her mouth to prevent it. We heard shouting and the barking of dogs; then there was quiet. No gunshots! The train started to move again and slowly gained speed.

I admired my brother's courage in escaping. He had the kind of quiet self-assurance I knew I could never have. I was thankful he was able to escape and trusted he had planned his strategy carefully. Years later, he told us what happened.

After Daniel jumped, he immediately rolled under the train and lay very still. When the Nazi guards, who hung onto the sides of the train, swept their flashlight beams underneath, he pulled himself up against the undercarriage. Fortunately, none of the guards dismounted to have a closer look. When the train started to move, he lowered himself down to the tracks and covered his head and chest with his attaché case to protect himself from low-hanging couplings. After the train passed over him he got up and hid in a ditch until darkness fell. He shaved off his beard because he knew that he looked more Jewish with it. Using the stars in the clear night sky as a guide, he headed south along the railroad tracks. He reached the Hooghalen train station in the early morning where he bought a paper and struck up a casual conversation with the ticket master in order to avoid raising suspicion. To his surprise, the entire Nazi contingent that had accompanied the train came into the station. He retained his composure and even talked to them about the weather! He took a train to Utrecht where he had lived and studied for many years. On the train he tried to decide whether he should walk or take the bus into town. He thought that more people would see him if he were on foot, but on the bus he would expose himself to closer scrutiny. He chose the bus and went to the apartment of Meta van der Velde, who was his girlfriend's sister. (His girlfriend had fled Holland for Indonesia, her birthplace, just before the occupation. Meta, who was two years older, was in her second year of studying pharmacology and wanted to stay in Holland.) My fiancé's brother, Johan, who was seventeen years old at the time, joined them, also seeking refuge. Being "half Jewish," Johan would probably not have been put in a death camp, but he was at risk of being sent to a labor camp in Germany.

Daniel did not leave this second-floor apartment for the next two years. He spent most of the time sitting behind an armoire that was placed diagonally across the corner of the room. At night he would sit in front of an open window to get fresh air. He did not step outside the apartment until 1944.

In September 1944, the British General Montgomery attempted Operation Market Garden, hoping to break through the German lines and liberate southern Holland by crossing the three rivers – the Maas, the Waal, and the Rhine. The Allied forces made it to Eindhoven where they were pushed back by German forces. Still occupied, northern Holland spent the winter with little food or fuel, as most had been confiscated by German authorities. Resources were so scarce that people had to burn their furniture and parts of their houses to keep warm. Even though there were food coupons, there was no food to buy. Some people preferred to get an extra ration of cigarettes rather than food because the need to reduce tension was more compelling than the need for nourishment.

The lack of food became so severe that at one point after spending three years indoors, Daniel and Johan decided to leave the haven of the apartment to barter with farmers who had food but needed clothing. It was not uncommon then for the citizenry to trade sweaters, socks or hats for beans, butter, or potatoes. Daniel had false identification papers acquired from the underground resistance movement. It was a dangerous trip and there were many checkpoints on the roads. Farmers who might seem willing to help could actually be Nazi collaborators. In addition, Johan was at an age that put him at risk of being forced to work in Germany. Armed with hope and pieces of clothing for trade, they set out on bicycles with wooden tires. (Rubber was in short supply and what there was had been taken by the Germans, so barrel-makers used wooden hoops as bicycle tires. It gave a very rough ride, but it worked.)

The trip took several days over rough cobblestone and unpaved roads. Daniel and Johan found a friendly farmer who let them stay in his barn and fed them oatmeal and milk. They made a trade and headed home with beans, bacon, and barley. On the way home, they were stopped by the Green Polizei who asked about the purpose of the trip and contents of their bags. Daniel, with a poker face, said, "Oh, a nice farmer gave me butter, eggs and bacon." The police officer thought he was joking and let them go.

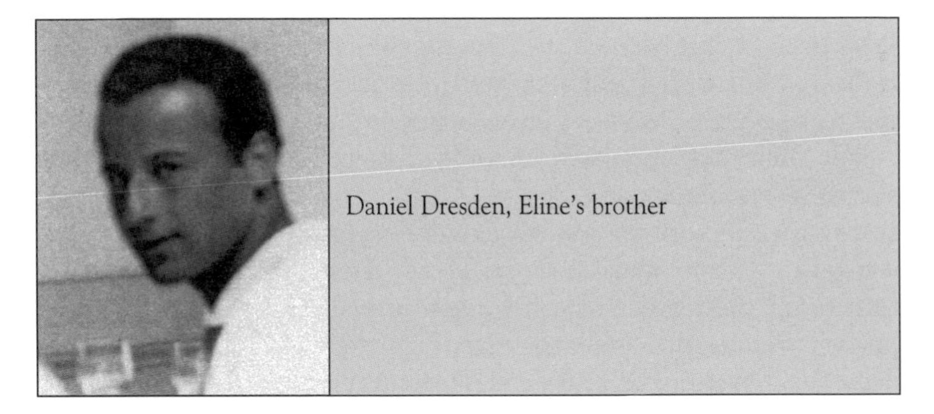

Daniel Dresden, Eline's brother

Daniel eventually married Meta and they had three children. He died of a heart attack in 1966, at the age of fifty-two. There was no history of heart disease in our family. I am convinced that his war experience took its toll on him.

Some years after the war, a high school friend named Rita told me her story of this time. She owned a crocheted bedspread, which she washed and then unravelled so she could use the yarn to knit socks to trade for food. There was a farm family who wanted all the socks she could make. It was a large family and she thought they needed lots of socks to wear with their wooden shoes. Coming to the end of her yarn supply, she had just enough left to make one last single sock. She presented it to the farmer with her apology for having only one and he said, "That's perfect! My wife has been making a bedspread from the yarn of the socks and she was short just a little bit."

* * * * * *

The Dutch government created the camp called Westerbork in 1939, in the northeastern part of the province of Drente, near the German border, as a central receiving place for Jewish refugees from Nazi Germany. On July 1, 1942, German officials seized the camp, surrounded it with guard towers and barbed wire, and thus it became an internment center for Jews on their way to the German death camps. The old, the sick, the young, including infants, all disappeared from it. Fifteen days after the Nazis took over the camp, the first train with 1,137 Jews left for the gas chambers.

We arrived at Westerbork in the early evening of September 28, 1943, after having been on the train for more than four hours. We were worn out, but with enough energy to be overcome with panic. There was to be no rest. We were given lukewarm "surrogate" tea and some bread. Then the entire eight hundred of us were made to stand in line all night for registration, a process that took about twelve hours. Because Westerbork was initially a refugee camp for German Jews, there were already many inmates there. These "senior" detainees were made to perform the registration of the new arrivals. They were dressed in prison coveralls with armbands that designated their function and were detached, devoid of emotion and almost robot-like in their demeanor. These were considered essential jobs, so good efficient performance gave the worker some measure of security. They sat at small tables with paper, pen and ink, some with typewriters. We were asked age, profession, former address, what vaccinations we had. The officials verified whether our names were on the lists as we claimed. We stood packed together, guarded by the S.S. and their dogs. Everyone leaned on each other. We lost our concept of time as we stood, half sleeping, dreaming of the past and future. Some people fainted and were left lying on the ground as relatives tried to tend to them.

The processing was finally completed the next morning. We were allowed to keep our combs and the clothes we were wearing, but our valuables such as watches, mirrors, etc. were taken and receipts issued with a promise of their later return. We were also given tickets to exchange for camp clothes and rations. Surprisingly, I was allowed to keep the riding boots that I wore. They had been made just for me when I went to college and took horseback riding and fencing. I felt they were a part of my identity and they gave me some sense of self-confidence.

My family was assigned to Barrack No. 85. We were instructed to be ready at seven o'clock in the morning for work detail. Beds were assigned. Beds were bunks, some with flea-infested straw mattresses, some with nothing. My bed was in the middle of a wobbling three-tiered iron bunk. Being short, I could sit upright in it. Later I traded with a woman for a top bunk. Even though the roof leaked on it, I preferred it because of the relative privacy it offered and I came to feel comfort at the sound of the rain above me. I was able to acquire a couple of nails and used them as hooks on which to hang things. These bunks constituted the only personal space we had. Everything I owned was kept on this bed. I could pretend it was my little attic room and it provided me with some refuge. I kept my beloved boots under my coat that I folded to serve as a pillow; I then folded myself into a secret little envelope of emotional protection into which I hid my hopes and fears and prayers. I had to be quick, though, because to dwell on such thoughts would have made me too weak to withstand the misery.

The complete lack of privacy, dignity, and pride was a salient feature of the crowded, stinking barracks. A barrack was about two hundred fifty feet long and thirty feet wide, with the entrance in the middle. To the left was the side for the women, to the right for the men. Tiered iron bunk beds lined the walls with a walkway in between. The children stayed with the women, but boys older than fourteen lived in the men's section. There was a large coal stove in each half of the building.

Westerbork was different from concentration and labor camps because the living conditions were better in many ways. We were allowed to have some contact, though limited, with the outside world and we could receive letters, packages, and food. We had some freedom of movement within the camp. There was a hospital that provided some skilled and dedicated medical care, but of course it lacked necessary medications, nursing equipment and surgical facilities. Fleas and lice were our constant companions. At night, what precious moments of sleep we could manage were ruined by the intense itching. The flea bites were the worst; the lice were confined to my head. My fingernails were broken and so I could not scratch very well. Each morning we combed the wretched, ragged sheets to hunt for fleas, which popped between our fingernails, spattering blood. I could catch about thirty or forty a day. We "groomed" each other's scalps, like monkeys, for lice and the person who found the most was triumphant. One of the harsh ironies was that the authorities tried to promote cleanliness by hanging up large posters with pictures of lice and fleas.

The only animals at the camp were the guard dogs, mainly Doberman Pinschers and German Shepherds, attack dogs used for the purpose of keeping us in line. I had cats when I was young and many of my friends owned dogs. The friendship of these animals enriched our lives, but in the harsh, god-forsaken place of Westerbork, we would not have had the emotional energy to give attention to an animal or receive the love of one. All our efforts were put into simple survival; there was no room for emotions other than fear.

The camp was hot and humid in the summer, cold and clammy in the winter. Because of many leaks in the building and the breath of so many people the humidity was always high. Each side of the barrack had one cracked, filthy toilet that was usually plugged up with rags that had been used for wiping. Each toilet was shared by four hundred people, all suffering from intestinal problems. No toilet paper or aids to basic hygiene were provided. A dirty curtain hung in front of the toilet to give the illusion of privacy. A trip to the barrack toilet was an exhausting and dreaded endeavor. Because there was no ladder, I had to step on the iron rails of the bed below mine and the rough edges cut into my feet. I remember the sounds of people vomiting as they made their way to the toilet. Often they cried as they tried desperately to hold the diarrhea until they could reach it. There was also an outhouse that was another source of the constant stench of excrement. Because it was outside, however, it was a little more tolerable. It was a red brick structure divided into two sides for men and for women. Inside was a long wooden plank with ten holes in it, laid over a boxed enclosure, forming multiple potties about a foot apart. There were no partitions to provide privacy. Actually, it afforded one the opportunity to visit with fellow outhouse patrons between attacks of diarrhea. The embarrassment of all this was outweighed by the need for compassion from fellow human beings and the comfort of a willing ear to listen to our worries. It was no small thing to hear encouraging rumors and some jokes to raise the morale. So, while getting to the outhouse through the cold, the mud and the rain was an ordeal, it sometimes felt worth the trouble to meet a friend. After living in the camp for awhile, some of us pried up a plank in the floor of the barrack and used the hole as a toilet. This was the level to which we were driven.

We lined up in the center of the barrack to collect our food. There was a half-hour window of time each morning to get food, otherwise, we had to do without. Breakfast was a slice of bread and a teaspoon of jam with brown water passing as coffee. Lunch often consisted of potatoes and cooked white cabbage. Sometimes there was a "goulash" with no meat. Food was brought from a main kitchen that cooked for the whole camp. By the time it reached our barrack it was lukewarm at best. We ate on tables between the bunks or while sitting on our beds. Supper was two slices of bread with a pat of margarine and the surrogate coffee. Food was often withheld in punishment. Whenever there was a fire in the stove, which happened only when the weather was freezing, we stuck our bread on the side of it and made toast.

Over the course of the war, two hundred and ten people escaped. After every escape, the camp commandant, Albert K. Gemmeker, retaliated by deporting ten residents from each barrack where the escape had taken place. This made us more scared but certainly not less determined to try to leave ourselves whenever we saw an opportunity.

My father, who was the leader for our barrack, was responsible for enforcing rules. One day he faced an embarrassing task. One of the rules was that the single toilet was to be used only during curfew hours at night. The outhouse was to be used at all other times. I remember the day Father saw a woman return from the barrack toilet. He politely reminded her of the rule to use the outhouse. The lady, a frail and sophisticated physician, pleaded her case by saying, "Professor, the aggregate of my relief deposited neither solids nor fluids in the toilet, so I felt that this would be permitted. I assure you, I used the toilet only as a place of isolation where I could get rid of gas! I do understand however, that there are rules, and I promise you it will not happen again". Of course, my father was just as embarrassed as she was and they came to the diplomatic agreement that there would be no punishment for breaking the rule. After the incident they were able to have a conversation about the health care conditions in the camp, and what to do about controlling contagious diseases. They also shared memories of our lives in Utrecht where they had both lived during peacetime. It was an oddly intimate discourse between strangers, one that no one ever could have imagined possible. The social rules guiding usual behavior had totally changed.

Every Tuesday and Thursday, the transport train departed, taking with it the individuals whose names had been called the previous night in the barracks at the hour of curfew. At the peak of the deportation from Westerbork, two to three thousand Jews were loaded onto the cattle cars of the train, eighty people per car. Each car held a large barrel to be used as a toilet. Men, women, children, the sick, the old, were all herded in together. Families were often separated from each other. There were no emotional outbursts, no weeping, only the yelling of the S.S. guards. Spirits were so diminished that resignation was all that was left. Experience had taught us that protestation only heightened the hardship.

Twice a week, month after month, the trains came and left with their human cargo. The event repeated itself over and over. The captives were numb with fear and hopelessness, totally overpowered by the guns, the dogs, the Nazis shouting, "*Schnell! Schnell!*" I believe that most of the people knew that the trains would carry them to more hard work, hunger, deprivation, illness, and death. But not one of us suspected that massive, systematized, industrialized murder was in store. We believed we were being sent to Germany to labor in camps. But there was growing apprehension that a more terrible fate lay waiting somewhere far away in East Germany.

* * * * * *

Westerbork was my home for one and a half years. I was fortunate not to be separated from my parents who were in the same camp. We were stripped of everything that our normal lives had to offer. The effort to get through another hour, another day, to come out the other end of this war with our lives, was all-consuming. Life was reduced to the most basic of motivations: stay alive! Through the worst of times, I cried no tears of sadness because I needed every atom of energy to survive. Kees was also held prisoner somewhere and our son was hidden with strangers. Life was so closely connected to death. Most of the people we loved the most were gone. We lived with an awareness of something horrible coming and it was terrifying to not know what that was. I somehow sensed that if I ever left Dutch soil, I had little hope of living. I had to try at any price to avoid being sent east to Germany. Even though we felt doomed, we did not protest. We did not want to do anything to increase our chances of being killed sooner rather than later.

Lagerkommandantur.

E. Dresden 4.1.23 Bar.: 85

soll sich am 1.4.44 um vorm. Uhr
bei der Lagerkommandantur melden.

Lager Westerbork, den 1.4.44

Büro Lagerkommandantur:
i.A.: Goldstein

Order for E. Dresden to report to the Camp Commander at specified date and time. These orders were stern in tone and caused much fear to inmates who had no idea why they were being summoned.

In February 1945, there was a sense of impending crisis in the camp. We thought that the war must be coming to an end and one not favorable to the Nazis. The many bombers flying over day and night made the ground rumble with a soothing sound, convincing us of the overwhelming powers of our allies. It was both frightening and encouraging. We thought about the old proverb, "a cat in narrow places makes funny jumps," when we wondered what our captors were going to do with us.

It was on the night of February 18, that Commander Gemmeker paid a visit to our barrack. After a three-hour inspection he concluded it was a pigpen. Indeed, it was filthy and it stank. He promised to be back in an hour and demanded that the place be spotless upon his return. He came back exactly on time with his entourage whereupon he and his black-booted thugs conducted another inspection. We had to stand in front of our bunks, erect and with expressionless faces, while they went through our shabby suitcases and in one, found two suits. They cursed at the owner, "Filthy Jew, you probably got rich in diamonds." They confiscated one suit and gleefully ripped up the other, looking for hidden diamonds sewn in the lining and making jokes with each other. Another one inspected the beds and was unhappy at how shabby they were. All we had were rags and old coats to use as covers. Gemmeker, enraged, pointed to some unpolished shoes, and promised to be back again in a couple of hours at which time he expected the shoes to get shined. Such a cruel joke it was. The shoes were so old and scuffed they were beyond polishing and we had nothing to use for polish anyway. The Nazis loved to heighten our fear by demanding the impossible. Everyone panicked, rushing from one end of the building to the other to find some polishing substance, maybe a little butter someone was hiding or some petroleum jelly they had smuggled in a long time ago. A rather pathetic job was done and we were all afraid of what would happen if Gemmeker were not satisfied with the results. What would be our punishment?

The Commander came back sooner than we anticipated. Some of us were still scurrying around to straighten up the place when the familiar yell came, *"Achtung, Herr Kommander Gemmeker!"* This time we had to parade in front of him and his cronies. When he decided that a pair of shoes did not look good enough, he took shoe polish and brush out of his pocket and proceeded to polish them himself. Occasionally he smiled at a child and ruffled his hair. Again, though, he was not satisfied and he "flunked" fifteen of the Barneveld-group women and fifty-eight of the men. He came back one more time, unannounced and alone. In anticipation of this, my father had already inspected everyone's shoes, hoping to avoid collective punishment. This time, sixty men did not pass – an interesting discrepancy of numbers. Gemmeker ordered all of these men to work heavy duty outside for two days, moving big sections of downed American airplanes to a location where they were to be disassembled and salvaged by women. After all this excitement, no one could sleep and another restless night finally ended with the whistle early in the morning.

One night, feeling cold and wet from a trip to the toilet, I fell into a light sleep. This time the unannounced inspection by the S.S. came, just ten minutes after I had fallen asleep. I dressed quickly, my clothes still damp from the day before when I worked in the woods. I found some dry paper to line my wooden shoes, as I had hidden my precious riding boots under a rag blanket so the authorities would not find them. I passed inspection but other individuals were forced to re-make their beds or were subjected to a random check for fleas or lice. Some were cited for having illegal food. Everyone was collectively punished for one person's infractions. The punishment was often late bread, no jam, no brown-water "coffee."

It was snowing and bitterly cold when I walked to the "*Apell*" field (location where roll call was taken) to join my work detail. On any particular day, several people might be absent, sick with influenza, strep throat or an infected wound. Some were weak from exhaustion and malnutrition, a dangerous condition to be in if one wanted to avoid being put on the train. We began chopping trees. Soon, we could not feel our hands and feet. They were like clumps hanging from the ends of our limbs, barely responding to our muscle commands. A one-armed soldier, who had been on the Russian front, tried to go a little easy by not pushing us and by keeping his dog by his side.

We worked hard all day. I was cold to the bone. My hands were swollen, my head ached and the pain in my shoulders was almost intolerable. I tried not to think. I continued to chop down trees about a foot and a half in diameter and carried them to a staging area where they were loaded on a small rail car. I was lucky to be well-connected; my father being a mechanical engineer was in charge of the tools, so I always had a sharp ax.

The trees were heavy and frozen. Wet overalls rubbed my skin raw as I waited for the end of the day and hoped to not get sick. I wondered what the next day would bring, but I knew the answer: more misery, more fear. My feet hurt and itched from frostbite, but my body still served me. At night I forced myself to think about Kees and Daantje, even though I didn't want to. I believed that if I did not think about them, something bad would happen to them. I devised a way to help me reserve my strength: I touched one finger to the spot on my hand where my wedding ring would have been in an attempt to unleash a power that would protect my loved ones. Each night, I crawled into that envelope of emotional refuge to recharge my courage and endurance.

It seemed to me that the women were generally more able to maintain some semblance of hope. Men stripped of their roles as breadwinners and protectors had no control over the fate of their family members. Totally powerless, they had no choice but to surrender. For many centuries, our culture had put Jews in a submissive state. They had to survive with their humor, their wit, and their faith. Those resources were hard to access now, yet we tried. One example of this involved my cousin, a professor of French literature and philosophy, who worked in the sewer system of the camp. One of his fellow workers, knowing my cousin's prowess with words, asked him to write a poem for his wife's birthday. Another example was the way that my mother discovered how to make pancakes with flour, water, and "candle fat." They were delicious and filling.

We tried to do a lot of laughing to stay sane so we made jokes about stupid Germans and smart Jews. Despite the tragedy around me, I never laughed so hard as I did in the camp. Keeping up our spirits was a critical survival requirement. We chose to believe good news and ignore the bad. We managed to find ways to inject some positive elements into our lives, however small.

The following joke made the rounds.

Hermann Goering, who was a high-ranking official in the German Nazi Party and close companion to Hitler, tried to convince Hitler not to kill all the Jews because they were smart and could be useful. Hitler didn't believe him, so Goering set out to prove it. He took Hitler to Berlin and went to a smoke shop to ask for some matches. The clerk handed some over, but Goering said, "The *Führer* wants them with the tips on the other end." The clerk apologized and said, "I'm sorry but I have only these." They left. Hitler said, "So, what does this prove?" Goering replied, "Be patient. We'll go to other shops." They did and always got the same answer. Finally they went to a Jewish shop and asked for the same thing. The Jew went into the back room, saying, "Just a moment, I'll be right back." A moment later he appeared and gave them a box of wooden matches with the tips on the other end. Hitler and Goering left the shop and Goering said, "See, I told you the Jews are smart!" to which Hitler replied, "No, no. The other shops probably just didn't have any of these!"

* * * * * *

Receiving mail helped us to endure as it established contact with the rest of the world and informed us that the sender was still alive. During our first few months in Westerbork, we were allowed to receive packages of food that weighed up to one kilo (about two pounds). All packages were inspected and stamped. We had to send the stamp to our friends who would then use the same stamp to send another package.

When Kees was living in Amsterdam with his brother, he sent packages containing sugar, margarine and eggs. The eggs were hard-boiled and packed in a yellow octagonal tin box with an elegant, hand-painted picture of a woman on the lid. Four eggs fit perfectly in it, forming a snug circle inside. This box became the egg shuttle and it survived the war, remaining in Amsterdam after the rule came that we could no longer receive packages. When Holland was liberated three years later, my brother-in-law gave it to me. I have had the precious little box for more than fifty years. It now holds brown sugar and has become a family treasure.

After my brother Daniel had escaped from the train, he learned its destination. Consequently, Meta van der Velde, the young woman who hid him, was able to send packages containing cookies and sugar or a little meat. Once she sent a package with sugar, honey, two hard-boiled eggs and crepes. The crepes were a delicious and nourishing treat, but we wondered why she took the trouble to make them. Years later, we learned that she had sent messages in them, on little pieces of paper carefully rolled up to fit in the pancakes. She wrote about my brother's escape and his being in hiding and what they did to pass the time in the anxious months. She wrote about Johan and his ability to go outside because he was a half-Jew. The messages, alas, were eaten! Later we were able to have a good laugh about it.

I was assigned to work outside and did various jobs, including chopping trees, unloading ships filled with rubble from bombed towns, digging up potatoes, and unloading freight trains bringing food to the camp. This last duty had the best potential for gain, as there was always something to steal if you dared to risk your life. I took the risk because of the defiance and personal triumph I felt, as well as the profit and power.

One day we had a trainload of onions to unload, so I took several. I put them in the front of my overalls and my rope belt kept them from dropping down into my pant-legs. As soon as I could, I hid them behind a wheel of the freight car and came back for them when it was dark. This was very risky because we were not allowed outside after curfew. I brought the onions to the barrack, so proud of my loot! We had never known how delicious a raw onion could be. I put them in a bedpan that my mother had taken from the hospital and hid it in my bed. I still have that white enamel bedpan with its long handle and wide-rimmed flat bowl. It is another one of the prized possessions I retain from that time.

Some days the work assignment was the unloading of a freight train with food for the German personnel. One day, it was hundreds of loaves of bread, still warm and smelling wonderful. I could not resist the temptation. I put four loaves behind a wheel of the freight car. That night I had special duty in the wash house and had permission to be out after curfew, so I retrieved the four loaves. Proud of my victory, I brought them to the barrack.

The next day, the authorities told us they knew there was a thief among us and my work crew was made to stand at attention for hours. We were told that if the culprit came forward, only he or she would be punished with hard labor; otherwise, the whole crew would be punished. I confessed. I had been subjected to hard labor before and I thought I could do it again, but I admitted to stealing two loaves, not four. I was ordered to return them. I worked extra hard for the next two days, but it was worth it. Despite the danger, it felt good to have fooled the enemy. When there was collective punishment everyone tolerated it. There was no energy to do otherwise. I can not recall that there was ever anger shown toward the person who violated rules and caused more hardship for the rest.

My mother worked in the hospital and in the kitchen. One day she stole some cauliflower and hid it in her apron. Meanwhile, I had taken a whole head from a freight car carrying vegetables. Taking advantage of the minimal supervision we had that day, I went back and got another

Painted tin box used as egg shuttle to and from Westerbork.

(Photo by Anton Dresden)

White enamel bedpan used to hide stolen onions in the barracks.

(Photo by Anton Dresden)

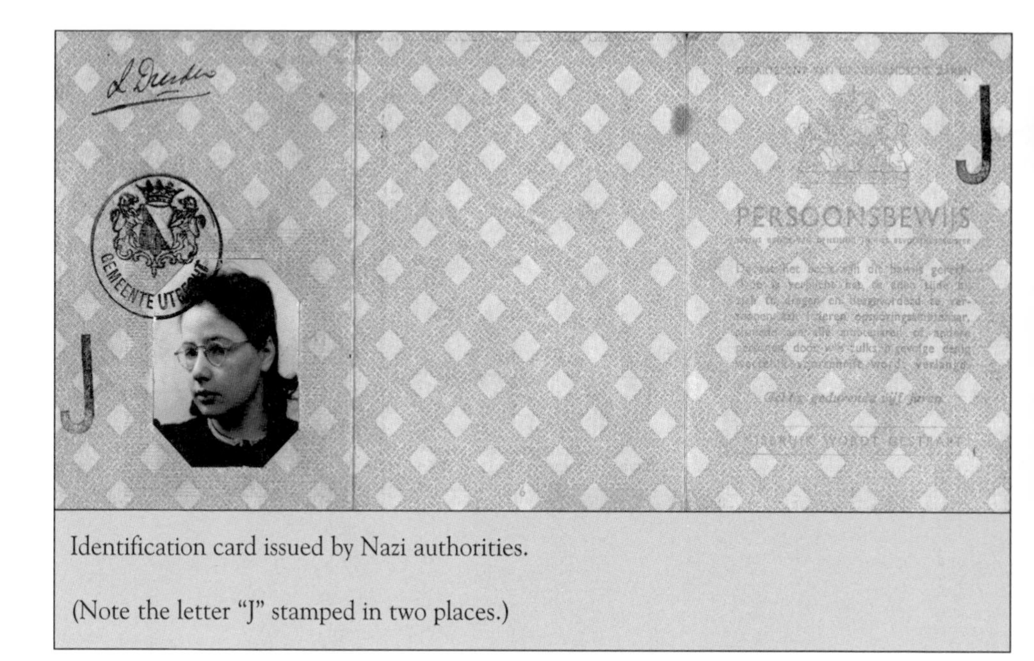

Identification card issued by Nazi authorities.

(Note the letter "J" stamped in two places.)

Inside of identification card.

one. That night we ate quite a bit of raw cauliflower, but we thoroughly enjoyed it. I hid the leftover amount in my top-tier bunk. After curfew, there was a knock on the door. I was afraid there was going to be an inspection. It turned out to be one of my father's helpers coming to surprise us with some cauliflower he had received from a friend. It was cooked! I don't know how they did it because we had no access to a source of heat and cooked cauliflower can be smelled a mile away, but we devoured it and laughed while we told him what we had done earlier. We were not caught and for days we had this wonderful vegetable. Its taste was enhanced because we had taken it from our captors.

One morning my work crew was planting peas. We put three peas in each hole, covered it with dirt and stomped it down with our wooden shoes. We planted row after row. Suddenly it dawned on me that there was a good chance that the war would be over by the time the peas sprouted, so I began to put just two peas in each hole, then one pea. Then I started skipping a few here and there. I decided to take the peas back to camp and try to find a way either to cook them or eat them raw. My father was assigned to the forge where there was a big stove that could be used to cook the peas. If it worked, it would be another victory. I put them in my coveralls and did not get caught. We cooked them that night in my father's workshop but my mother was too scared to eat them because the German authorities had told us that they were poisoned in an attempt to keep us from stealing them. My father and I ate a few peas first, with no ill effects, so then we gorged ourselves on them. It is one of my favorite memories. After we were liberated I looked at the pea field and it was pathetic indeed. There were many empty spots.

I harvested vegetables, including sugar beets, potatoes, and cabbages. The cold and the frost made the potatoes mealy and soft. Our stiff, almost frozen hands would occasionally push into a rotten potato, making it spurt into our faces. Once in awhile I was able to steal a good potato. We sliced it thinly and stuck the slivers onto the barrack stove to make a primitive potato chip, lacking only the salt. This invention was a major treat. Sugar beets were one of the best things to steal. In the morning we took wheelbarrows and burlap sacks to load the vegetables and at night we sometimes returned to camp with a few unfilled bags. Sometimes I was able to smuggle beets under these bags. In my father's shop, we cooked them for a long time until they became like syrup or a rich molasses. We had to be careful to keep the pot covered to minimize the chance that cooking odors would escape. Driven to steal in order to survive, we did it well. These small victories kept us going.

The work detail gave us opportunities to obtain extra food through dangerous but rewarding means. On one occasion I got something extra-special by accepting a dare. My crew was sorting vegetables in a cold, dim underground cellar. Once a month, the vegetables were rotated, which meant that sometimes we had to handle rotten matter that had become slimy and disgusting. The smell was nauseating. Talking was prohibited, but we did it anyway. One woman, whose husband worked in the butcher shop in the camp, challenged someone to eat two mouthfuls of cabbage slime in exchange for a half-inch piece of liverwurst. Thrilled at the thought of bringing liverwurst back to my parents, I did it. All eyes watched as I chewed and swallowed, though little chewing was required. I didn't vomit, although I wanted to for several hours afterward. The liverwurst was heavenly. My parents were delighted with it and talked about it for weeks.

It was difficult to have an accurate sense of time as the days went by slowly. They seemed an endless torture. On the ground behind the barrack, my father had laid out a crude sundial for me made out of pebbles and a piece of wood. It made me feel good and it gave me a sense of control. To this day, I have a special fondness for sundials.

In the early months of our internment, we were allowed to send a letter once a week and to receive a two-pound package each month. I wrote to Kees that my father had a bad cold. He wrote back that he would send medication for it. We were disappointed to find that the next package we got contained a bottle of cough syrup. My father, however, was gracious and said, "How attentive of Kees." But he knew that I was embarrassed that my fiancé would foolishly waste the precious two-pound allowance on cough syrup. I couldn't understand why Kees had done did this. When we opened the bottle, we discovered that it was filled with gin. Kees had resealed the bottle so well that the authorities didn't catch on. Everyone was happy and Kees was vindicated. Another victory! It was greatly appreciated because the following weeks were especially cold and we could enjoy a sip of gin before going to bed.

Several weeks later we got a package containing a bottle of ketchup. This time we knew what it was before we opened the bottle and we were right. These triumphs were sweeter than any accomplishment because they represented some measure of successful resistance to the evil that surrounded us. It was a wonderful way to make us feel connected to the outside world and it strengthened my bond with Kees, who showed the imagination I knew we had in common.

* * * * * *

When I first arrived at the camp I was assigned to work in the camp's hospital. It was a building with bunk beds like the other barracks. There was no medical equipment, no linen, no supplies. If a patient in an upper bunk had diarrhea, it would drip down to the bed underneath. I could not bear to work there so when a request for outside workers was made, I was glad to volunteer.

The "Outside Commando" was a group of ten to fifteen camp inmates who were taken beyond the camp environs to work under the supervision of armed S.S. officers and their guard dogs. Working outside the camp had many advantages, if one was strong enough to survive the elements dressed only in coveralls without underwear and wooden shoes that caused painful bunions on the front of the foot. It was extremely important to be healthy and tough to be put on the outside work detail. The days were long and the labor was hard. Sometimes we received extra rations. But the best reason to be on this crew was the sense of freedom I felt getting past the gate in the early morning, despite the guards who accompanied us, ready to shoot anyone who tried to run. (Our clothing was designed to make running difficult.) Here on the outside the sky seemed higher, the air seemed fresher, and, most importantly, we could not see the sinister, ever-present railroad tracks that were a constant reminder of the threat of deportation.

One day, with hours of hard labor ahead of us, we marched to the work site under a cloudless sky. The nice weather was something of an omen. That afternoon we heard airplanes, Allied forces returning from a mission. Their purpose was to protect low-flying bombers, but after the bombers had completed their missions, the protector planes could look for targets on their own. In the distance we saw several fighters strafe a German train three times until it was stopped. It was a thrilling event for us to witness, almost as if we were watching a scene from a movie. We returned to our work with renewed diligence. The fighter planes returned however, and fired on Camp Westerbork. We were afraid for our relatives still in the camp.

That evening we received news of what had happened at the camp. A few people were hurt, but no one was killed. My mother, who had been sick in bed that day, felt a bullet just miss her head. A dress that I had hung on a nail was riddled with bullet holes. I kept it for many years after the war.

Watch tower at Camp Westerbork

Drawing by Ed Strelitski *De Beul Regeert* (*The Hatchet Man Rules*) written by Daniel Dresden and published in 1945 by De Hofstad DenHaag

On some days, the guards took the work crew to unload ships on a canal one and a half kilometers from the camp. The road was graveled, muddy and full of potholes. Often the weather was bitterly cold, foggy and dark, reflecting the mood of our tired, despondent group, comprised mostly of women. The canal accommodated large barges, often filled with rubble from bombed Dutch cities and towns. Our task was to unload the debris, consisting of marble, wood, brick and metal, into containers that were the size of a modern-day oval laundry basket. One person got into the hull of the barge and filled the basket; then it was handed up through a receiving line two or three persons deep until it reached the top. It was back-breaking, exhausting work and many women collapsed under the weight of the baskets. Our hands were frozen, making it hard to hold the handles as bricks fell out and hit us. The guards constantly shouted out, "*Schnell! Schnell!*"

It helped to be able to establish a rhythm in passing the containers. The debris was carried away in tip-cars, such as the ones used in coal mines, then broken down with sledgehammers. The end product was used to improve dirt roads. I thought about the once-proud marble pillars and beautiful sidewalk tiles that were now reduced to stone crumbs by women who perhaps used to live around them.

When the weak gave up, we were not allowed to help them. They were usually herded off to stand for the rest of the day, surrounded by the guard dogs. It often meant that they would be put on the next train. When a person died on the site, we pushed them back to the camp at night in a wheelbarrow.

As part of the "outside" work crew, I was sometimes ordered to perform the duties of inmates who were sick. A couple of times I had to burn the bodies of individuals who were shot while trying to escape, or the bodies of those who died from disease or "old age." The camp had two coal-burning ovens for this purpose.

The building that housed the ovens was dingy and poorly lit. The ovens themselves were round like large tubes and made of brick. The first time I was assigned to this duty, it was a cold, blustery winter day. The wind howling outside underscored the macabre nightmare that it was. I had to use my rationality to get through this task, so I told myself that the individuals who had lived and suffered in these bodies were gone. Their loved ones were either suffering as they had or were gone too. I could not be of help to any of them. I had to dissociate myself from feelings of horror and sorrow in order to complete this assignment and go on with life. Aided by these coping mechanisms, I was able to complete the task without feeling scared, upset, or nauseated as one might expect. I shoved the body of an older man strapped to a gurney-like apparatus, into the waiting oven, closed the round door and turned the latch. The door had a window in it, similar to a porthole on a ship. The thought occurred to me that I had put the person on a journey over the sea of life, vanishing into the horizon, into the "heavens."

Having never done a thing like this before, I could not have foreseen what happened next. The heat of the fire caused the tissues and tendons to react, making the body move and look as if it had come alive and were trying to get out. Of course this added to the eerie, unreal, dreamlike quality of the whole scene. After it was over, I found out that I had earned a shot of gin and a slice of liverwurst. This was the reward the Nazis gave us, knowing that this would soften our disgust of our task. I shared these treats with my parents and anticipated them the next time. Such are the merits of war.

Sanitation was extremely poor in the hospital. While working there, my mother was exposed to germs and bacteria. In the morning, two people carried hot water in large galvanized tubs from the water-heating plant to the hospital. By the time it arrived there, half of the water had spilled out and the remaining half was tepid. Soap was so scarce that most of the time, it was non-existent. Although the floors were mopped with Lysol every day, the overcrowded clinic always stank and contagious diseases were prevalent. Rags were used for sheets and as bandages. Once in a while, when a transport arrived from another hospital, we got some gauze.

Mother injured her hand while working in the kitchen and a cut on her middle finger grew into a nasty infection, swollen and red. After several days, it turned bluish red and swelled to double its size, causing the skin to tear. She was in terrible pain and could not use her hand at all. She developed a high fever and the red lines going up her arm to her shoulder were a sure sign of blood poisoning. I took her to the hospital where the doctor had to resort to a drastic, excruciating treatment. Luckily we had an abundance of excellent doctors. A surgeon made cuts in her finger between all three joints, then stuffed the end of a long strip of cotton gauze in the cuts. Several times a day he pulled the gauze a little and it absorbed the fluid and pus until it finally was pulled all the way through. No painkillers were to be had, and Mother endured it bravely. Miraculously, her finger was saved. After a few anxious days, the infection localized, the fever broke and she returned to her work assignment. I admired her courage, her determination and her strong constitution.

* * * * * *

The inmates of Westerbork were required to assist in the loading of the trains carrying fellow inmates to Germany. Their fates were not explicitly known, but were known, on some level, in our hearts and minds. Each train carried about 2,500 people. It left twice a week, every Tuesday and Thursday, until 1944, when it was reduced to once a week, on Tuesdays only. We heard the train arrive during the night with the squeaking noise of the change of the main track to the one entering the campground. Of course no one could sleep, and people searched around for some extra clothes and packed their satchels with their meager belongings. The inmates who were chosen for this loading task belonged to the Outside Commando. This was the crew that performed most of the hard labor of loading, chopping trees and working in the fields, but of all these duties, helping our fellow Jewish victims into the waiting cattle cars with their dark gaping holes was the worst of all.

The smell of pea soup in the air foretold the approach of a dreaded transport. For some unknown reason, it was cooked for these occasions. The odor, mixed with the stench of unwashed bodies, raw sewage, vomit and fear, was nauseating and caused a sense of panic. Perhaps the soup, with its disastrous intestinal effects, was chosen to enhance the hardship for those being stuffed into the cattle cars. There was an oil barrel for a toilet, and another for drinking water. There was nowhere to sit or lie down; there was only the desire to make your loved ones comfortable with a loving arm around the shoulder or a lap to sit in, a whisper of "I love you" in an ear and a loving look.

I was assigned to transport duty for a particular Tuesday, sometime between 1943 and 1944. Every one was scared and the mood in the barracks was very tense, causing people to argue among themselves. No one knew that the train was bound for Auschwitz, and even if they had known, they had no idea what that would mean. I wore a special white armband with big black letters *"O.D."* (*Order Dienst*) which indicated that I was on the loading crew. I saw a mother who tried to hand her baby (about the age of my son Daantje) to one of my colleagues, hoping to save it from a frightening future. One of the S.S. officers came with his dog and told the man to give the baby back to the mother who was quietly weeping. I quickly looked away, feeling sick to my stomach. It was raining and the woman and her baby were drenched. She entered the boxcar. At least it was dry in there, I thought, and the people already inside surely would try to comfort her.

One of the women with an *O.D.* band like mine fainted and was carried away. I stood still, watching, then felt a shove in my back. It was a Nazi yelling "*Schnell! Schnell!*" at me. I saw an older woman and her husband, probably in their late sixties, walking arm in arm to the train. The woman looked old, tired and scared. He was older than she, but still protective and encouraging to his lifelong partner. They seemed painfully frail as they tried to comfort each other, ready to board the dark windowless boxcar, so cold and stinking and filled with the unspoken promise of death. Until now, life had taught them that they could face anything together. They trusted that they could get through this hardship together as well.

The old man held his wife's elbow as they walked, guiding her through the crowd. It was a sweet, tender gesture of love and devotion. The heavy suitcase he carried made him lean to the side, emphasizing his frailty. She carried a small overnight bag and held her head high. Suddenly the man slumped to the ground. A Green *Polizei* kicked him in the stomach to make him get up. He did not move. The wife stroked his head and pleaded for help. She knelt beside him, but the police pulled her up by the arm, yelled at her and kicked her as well. She swayed on her feet, the tears running down her cheeks. The grey-uniformed S.S. pushed her with the butt of his rifle into the boxcar where she leaned against the wooden latch, her sad, loving eyes following her husband's body.

The camp police was summoned to load the crumpled body of her husband into a wheelbarrow. His suitcase was thrown on his face. The wife stretched out her hand to touch his body one last time, her eyes filled with horror. She cried silently and whispered his name. An extra push with the gun and the scene was over. I tried to come close to the car to say a few words of comfort to her. The *Polizist* laughed and told me to shut up as he lit a cigarette and inhaled deeply.

The boxcar doors closed and the train moved forward for a short way, stopped, backed up, and sat for about fifteen minutes. All of a sudden Camp Commander Gemmeker and a few of his officers walked up to the train, opened boxcar Number 21 and called a name. A man was told to get out. He looked stunned but happy. In the meantime an officer came with another inmate who was thrown in the black gaping hole of the opened door. The door was slammed shut. Maybe the man who was replaced had found a way to get off the transport list, and since the required quota had to be met, another body had to fill his place.

This occasionally happened and was the reason why no one could feel relieved not to be on a transport until the train had actually left the camp. The doors closed again and the train slowly pulled out, leaving for good, we thought; however, it stopped, came back again. A mechanism was uncoupled and agonizing minutes passed. Then it moved, picked up speed and left the camp. The whistle blew like so many train whistles throughout the world, throughout time.

I went to get my pea soup, the reward of the day, thinking about the elderly couple loving each other until death. The scene was forever etched into my soul.

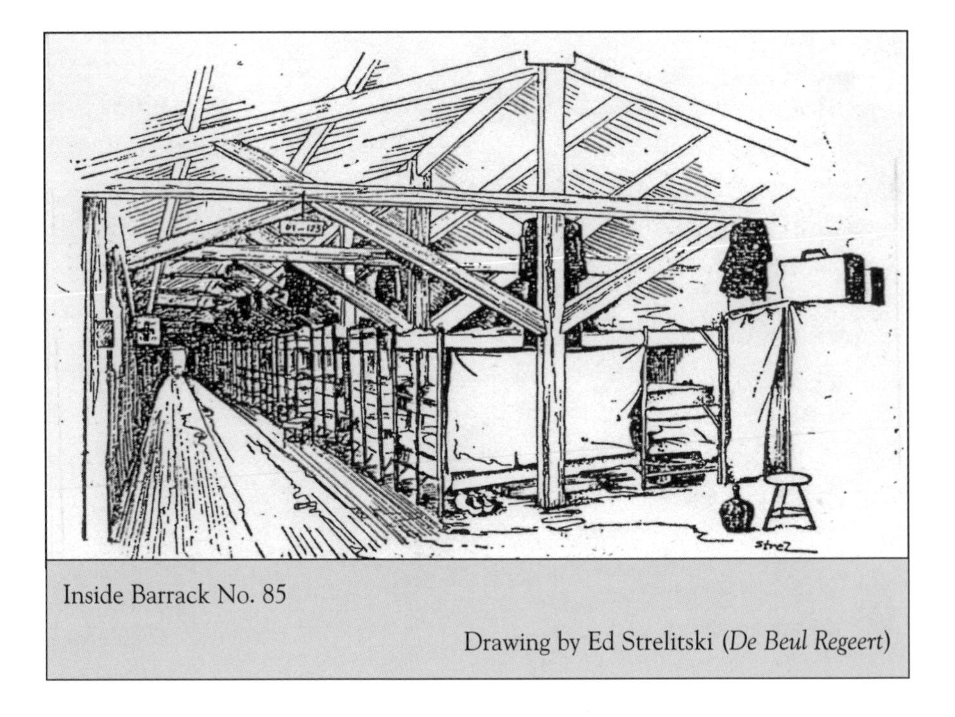

Inside Barrack No. 85

Drawing by Ed Strelitski (*De Beul Regeert*)

View of barrack 84 from barrack 85

Drawing by Ed Strelitski (*De Beul Regeert*)

Chapter 4

HOW IT ENDED

On September 3, 1944, a train left Westerbork with four hundred ninety-eight men, four hundred forty-two women, and seventy-nine children on board. It was different from other trains because it included all of the patients in the hospital and all of the children in the camp, with and without their parents. I was working on transport duty, wearing the armband designating my exemption, and carrying the *ausweis*, a document that showed proof of my responsibilities. The train's destination, though we did not know it at the time, was Auschwitz. Anne Frank and her family were on this train. She had been staying in the "punishment" barrack, one that housed Jews who were caught while in hiding. They arrived in Westerbork in early August after being caught in an *achterhuis* (the back of a house) on the *Prinsegracht* in Amsterdam. From Auschwitz, she was transported to Bergen-Belsen where she died. I do not remember seeing her at Westerbork, but I feel that I knew her from her diary and I regard her as a symbol of so many budding young women who never got to live out their lives.

Found after the war. Train sign from Camp Westerbork

(photo by Faith Yang)

Baptized Jews and the "elite" group (including the Intellectuals) that had been at Barneveld were scheduled for our final journey on September 4th, destined for Theresienstadt in Czechoslovakia. My mother had used flour, water, and candle fat to make pancakes on an unoccupied burner in the kitchen where she worked. We planned to hide them in our clothing. The ominous smell of pea soup was already in the air.

6.45 Uhr bei F.K. melden
Ausweis
(ist auch als Nachtausweis gültig)
Der Lagerinsasse Dresden, Eline
geboren: 4.1.23 Baracke: 38
hat am 3 SEP. 1944 194 Dienst beim
abgehenden/ankommenden Transport.
Der Dienstleiter:

Notice of Eline's transport duty on September 3, 1944. This was one of the last two trains to leave from Westerbork. It took Anne Frank to Auschwitz.

I sensed that leaving The Netherlands would mean death. I was desperate to find a way to stay in Westerbork, but Father said that it was impossible, that everyone had to go. I found out that a few people had been allowed to stay because their status as a Jew was in question. For example, a full Jew who had a child with a non-Jewish spouse could be exempt from deportation. This made me think that exceptions were made, so why not try? My father and I went to see the highest-ranking Jewish official in the camp. We were armed with several arguments: Father was in charge of technical services; my mother worked in the hospital; I was a good manual laborer; the camp would be needed as a place of retreat for German soldiers and our skills would enable this little city to continue to function. We begged, pleaded and argued our case. We were denied exemption.

We went back to the barracks to continue preparations for departure the next day. We were told to paint our names and birth dates on our rucksacks. As I sat and waited, I was wearing my beloved riding boots. The curfew hour had come and we felt trapped and frightened. Midnight passed. At two o'clock in the morning there was a knock on the door. A messenger from the commandant told us that we were staying in Westerbork and we were to report for duty immediately. Twenty people from the Intellectuals list and twenty people from the

Baptized list were chosen to remain, the result of a concession by German authorities to political groups in The Netherlands.

Father was overjoyed. Mother ate one of the pancakes and gave the rest to friends who had to go. I was so relieved for us that it overshadowed my sadness for the others. The next day, the train with a thousand Jews including the Intellectuals and the Baptized Lists left for Theresienstadt.

Theresienstad was a concentration camp where gas chambers were being built but were not finished in time to be used. Most people who died there were either shot at random when some punishment action took place or succumbed to one of the many diseases. Many people left from there for Auschwitz and other camps all over Germany and Poland.

The last train departed from Westerbork on September 13, 1944, headed for Bergen Belsen. There were about two hundred eighty individuals on board. Some were people who had been caught in hiding,

Ausweis

An Dresden,Daniel

geb.2o. 1.86 Bar. 38

Sie gehen nicht mit dem Transport vom 4.9.44.

Dieser Ausweis ist unbedingt mit sich zu fuehren.

Der Dienstleiter

D.B.1

3.9.44

Notice to Daniel Dresden that reads: "You are not going on the transport of September 4, 1944. This notice must be kept with you at all times."

but most were old camp inmates, many of whom were German Jews who had arrived there before the German occupation of The Netherlands. They had been spared for so long by virtue of their seniority, but ironically met their deaths so very close to the end of the war. Miraculously, some of the camp inmates on our missed train survived the transport to Theresienstadt and made it through the war. Years later, they told us that my mother's pancakes sustained them.

September 5, 1944, was known as *Dolle Dinsdag* ("Crazy Tuesday") in Holland. The south of Holland had been liberated and people thought that the war would soon be over and the Nazis would leave. The citizenry's hatred of the Nazi collaborators found expression in acts against them. Male collaborators were beaten and marched through the streets in their uniforms. Young women who had consorted with Nazis had their heads shaved. Many of these collaborators tried to flee from the cities and seek refuge among the Jews. In our camp, these *N.S.B.* members were protected by the camp commander and were treated as guests. We, the inmates, were ordered to take care of them, providing them with clothing, food, and shelter. I saw a woman sitting on a suitcase, looking sad and complaining about what a mess she was in. She said that she used to have such a good life in a nice villa that had been taken from Jewish owners. Her husband said that they would be better off by joining the Nazi movement. She thought I would feel sorry for her.

Almost half a year went by after the last transport train left on September 13, 1944. We did not know it would be the last one. A small train with regular passenger cars sat on the track in the camp for six months, constantly threatening us like a crocodile waiting to snap us up. It remained there until the end.

We knew the end of the war was near. The German forces had obviously run out of supplies. We saw old men on bicycles ride by, carrying bazookas over their shoulders. Allied airplanes constantly flew overhead. Every day, all day, we saw low-flying bombers and fighter planes going east, and on the other side of the sky we saw the empty bombers returning. The fighter planes continued to complete their side missions, strafing trains and trucks. As a result, the railroads were in bad shape, causing curtailment in transportation for the German forces. There were about four hundred of us left in the camp. We were in relatively good health; had we been unhealthy we would have been deported. Some of the inmates had been caught while in hiding and were brought to Westerbork to be transported, but they were lucky. The trains were no longer running. Those of us still there kept the camp functioning by running the kitchen, the hospital, the sewer, and the water system because the camp might be needed for German troops on the retreat. We didn't know what the Nazis planned for us. After enduring these difficult years in the camp, how was it going to end for us? Would we be marched into the fields and shot? I remember living these weeks with that fear of the unknown that had descended on me so many times before.

On New Year's Eve, 1944, I was on night duty, patrolling the camp while my mother worked at the hospital. It had been five long years of war for Holland. I carved the words *Gelukkig Niew Jaar* ("Happy New Year") out of a carrot. I took it to the hospital where my mother and I ate a few of the letters. I re-carved those we had eaten and took them to my father and he and I celebrated again. It was a small gesture that did a lot to raise our spirits.

At the end of March 1944, we heard a rumor from farmers on "the outside" delivering goods to the camp that Canadian troops were on the other side of the canal about a mile and a half away. The camp was unusually quiet; something was in the air. On the eleventh of April, we awoke to a strange sight. The guard towers, usually manned with soldiers and machine guns, were empty. Artillery fire grew louder as low-flying fighter planes swept over the camp. The Germans were gone.

We did not dare to let ourselves feel happy yet, but how we wanted to! Some people decided to leave, not really sure where to go. My father was elected to lead us. He warned those who wanted to leave that they were in danger of being hit by friendly fire. There was no means of transportation and collaborators still posed a great danger. Four people left. As the day wore on we became more anxious. We went to sleep for a few hours, got up and wondered, discussed, speculated. More restless hours passed.

On the morning of April twelfth, we awoke to a rumbling so loud that the ground shook. We ran to the gate. In the distance we saw Canadian Sherman tanks emerge from their clouds of dust. It was an unbelievable sight. I felt my flesh rise and my heart race with joy. What a mixture of emotions surged through us – elation, apprehension, gratitude, anxiety about our loved ones, rage at our mistreatment! We shouted out with joy and waved wildly to our liberators. We must have alarmed them because they closed their hatches until they were close enough to see who we were. I imagine we were a deplorable sight. Some of us had shaved heads and filthy clothing. We were all screaming wildly. The Canadian soldiers greeted us with warmth and compassion, giving us chocolate and cigarettes.

The war situation was not clear. It was not over, but the Allies were clearly winning. Most of the tanks proceeded north to Groningen, the next big city. I watched my mother standing on the dirt road, waving to the soldiers as they passed by, another scene from the drama that was our lives.

No. Identity card: WESTERBORK CAMP
(Identiteitsbew.) KAMP WESTERBORK
No. 22
Only valid: day of issue -----
(alleen geldig: dag v. uitg.)
valid till : 1 Juni 1945
geldig tot) :
Mr./Mrs. Daniel Dresden
is allowed with ------ men
(heeft toestemming met pers.)
to leave / to enter the camp.
(het kamp te verlaten/te betreden)
Reason: verlof naar Eindhoven voor
(Reden) belangrijke besprekingen
Westerbork, 26 Mei 1945
Recommended: Approved
(initials only)
De Militaire Commissar
Superintendent Allied Milit. Comm.
Expired passes are to be returned to the office for cancellation.
(de vervallen passen moeten onmiddellijk op het uitgiftebureau ingeleverd worden.)

Pass given to Daniel Dresden after Liberation allowing him to come and go from Camp Westerbork.

We had not yet regained control of our lives, but we were no longer hunted and persecuted. My father and I went back to our duties. A few tanks stayed to guard the camp, forming a circle around it, much like the wagon trains of the old American West. We watched as the soldiers dug holes, almost deep enough for a person to stand in. They poured gasoline in the holes and lit them. They did not communicate with us very much and we had no idea what they were doing. Our conditioned skepticism made us wonder if these soldiers were Germans in disguise intending to burn us to death one by one. Soon, however, it became clear that they were heating water for tea. Not even war could interfere with a Canadian's afternoon tea!

The Canadian officer who took charge of Westerbork was Captain Morris. His responsibilities were to keep order, monitor those who came in under false pretenses, and such. He appointed my father to help solve daily problems. I remember that after the camp was liberated, we were given cans of corned beef with little folding can-openers that came with food rations. I carry mine in my purse to this day.

Anton Mussert, the head of the Nazi Party in Holland, was arrested on May 7, 1945, in The Hague and was executed exactly one year later.

* * * * * *

After Westerbork was liberated, refugees began to arrive, seeking shelter and protection among the Jews still there. After a few days, the Canadian soldiers asked us to register all arriving persons. If we felt the least bit suspicious, we were to frisk them, strip-search them and check their bags. The Canadians' caution was well-founded. Many of the newcomers were discovered to be collaborators or members of the *Nationale Socialistische Beweging*. They brought with them all kinds of Nazi paraphernalia, including S.S. emblems, medals of honor, or photographs of their Nazi boyfriends or girlfriends. Many of the items had been sewn into the linings of women's purses or undergarments. Some even had swastikas tattooed on their breasts.

When a collaborator was caught he or she often had a "sob story" to tell. They begged, pleaded, and cried. I considered myself a civilized and humane person, but I must admit to feeling pleasure when I succeeded in exposing one of them. I savored the challenge of using my resourcefulness and intelligence to uncover the proof of their loyalty to the Nazi movement. I examined their purses, throwing the contents on the table, and did not care if their tubes of lipstick or their lockets containing baby hair or any other treasures rolled to the ground. My hands were adept at detecting any stiffness in the flaps of their handbags, indicating the presence of a hidden picture of their "hero," and after I emptied their purses, I felt satisfaction in ripping up the lining, just the way the fabric of our lives had been torn to shreds by our persecutors.

These were people who had voluntarily carried out the commands of their Nazi cohorts, no matter how cruel the task. They did it with pleasure, hoping for a wonderful career with the Third Reich. I am not proud of the satisfaction and enjoyment I felt ripping apart purses and tearing off brassieres. Abel Hertzberg, a Dutch Jew, wrote the book, *It is Hidden In All of Us*, that describes the hate, vengeance and disdain we are all capable of feeling for another human being. That phenomenon was never so clear to me as during those moments I spent with the members of the *N.S.B.*

Kees had been imprisoned in Berlin for stealing leather to repair his shoes. In early April 1945, Russian soldiers rammed the doors of the jail with tanks and broke through. The prison population included political prisoners, criminals, and people picked up for theft or other violations. The prisoners were ecstatic and began to sing the international song of liberation. The Russian soldiers gave them food from the prison kitchen and butchered animals from the prison farm for meat. They warned the inmates, some of whom had been there for a long time, not to eat too much because their digestive systems needed to adjust; however, there were those who did not heed the warning and died from complications related to this.

Kees left within a couple of days and set out on foot toward Holland, four hundred kilometers away. Sometimes he had to use crutches because he was so weak, and he hitchhiked a good part of the way. Confusion reigned. The country was in chaos. People often had no identification papers. One was careful to not ask too many questions. Two strangers joined him and the three travelers arrived at a British army camp. One of the strangers was discovered to be a Nazi officer attempting to flee in order to escape punishment. The British soldiers assumed that all three were S.S. and prepared to execute them but a high-ranking officer stopped the firing squad because there had been no investigation. Kees was saved. Despite liberation and the end of the war, safety was not guaranteed.

Kees became sick with pneumonia, but continued to travel on. It took him days to get to the province of Limburg in southern Holland. He arrived at a receiving center that provided food and shelter for repatriates. It is hard to describe how massively chaotic the situation was during this time. The Red Cross had obtained lists of the names of people in the internment camps. I had typed such lists of survivors of Westerbork. It was on one of these lists that Kees found my name and the names of my parents. We had not had contact for three years. We did not even know if the other were still alive. Kees hitched a ride on a truck going north to deliver coal and retrieve dairy products. Unexpectedly, he showed up at Westerbork and joined us. I still feel my stomach jump when I recall what it was like to see him alive and well after more than three years filled with terror and brutality.

We stayed at Westerbork for another two months. Our identities had to be checked and cleared and the authorities had to be convinced that we had a place to live. Finally, we were allowed to leave the miserable place that had been our involuntary home for three terrible years. In the end, nine hundred Jews were released from Westerbork.

* * * * * *

My father had always said that we would go home on a Tuesday, and sure enough, my brother, Daniel, showed up on Tuesday, June 5, 1945, with a flatbed truck to take us home. We left the next day, on Wednesday, so Father was close. Right after our liberation in April, we had searched the abandoned officers quarters of the camp looking for information that could be useful to us. In the quarters, I found a few pieces of furniture from my bedroom, including two chairs and an armoire with a mirror. Our names and address were still on the back panel of the armoire. What a joyful feeling it was, to see part of home! We took the furniture back to Utrecht with us. The armoire fell apart years ago, but I have the chairs and the mirror with me today. I have never considered getting rid of them.

Daniel and Meta had married a few months before the end of the war. When we arrived in Utrecht, we had no house, so we lived with them in their third floor apartment along with another family that was staying there as well. The apartment building was on a street familiar to us – we had ridden our bicycles on it many times on the way to and from school. On our return, friends who had stored our possessions for us said that their servants had taken them. Although they apologized, they reminded us to be grateful that we had survived. A year later, we attended the wedding of the daughter of one of these "friends." We were surprised to see our linens, crystal, and other valuables being used at the reception. The poor handyman with nine children, however, immediately returned our wedding rings. The infamous soap dispenser, that precious symbol of defiance, was recovered. It found its home later in my parents' house in Delft, hanging on the wall above a basin in the corner, and I always looked upon it with tremendous pleasure.

Dient Bureel Kampintendant .

Heeren Kamppolitie
en
Bewakingstroepen N.B.S.

Den heer Hoofdbarakkenleider
Korman en
Barakkenleiding .

Den Heeren Daniel Dresden geboren 14-6-1914 en
den bestuurder Nederhof , is vergunning
verleend hedennacht in het kamp te overnachten .
Er wordt verzocht hen van eten te willen voorzien
(ook brood , boter enz.) door hen op te nemen in de
melding van het eten van 5 en 6 Juni 1945 .

Kamp Westerbork , 5 Juni 1945 De Kampintendant
op last

onze Daan en een chauffeur v. een
vrachtwagen uit Utrecht die onze
Daan gecharterd had om ons terug
te halen,

Pass that reads: "Mr. Daniel Dresden, Jr. born June 14, 1914, and the Chauffeur Nederhof are granted permission to stay overnight tonight in the camp. It is requested that food be furnished for them (also bread, butter, etc.) by including them in the call for meals on June 4 and 6, 1945."

Chapter 5

REUNION AND RECOVERY

Kees and I went to s'Graveland where our son, Daantje, lived in hiding. We had hoped to stay for a few days to allow him to get used to us. When we arrived, Nel Vermey, his war mother, asked us to take him immediately as her attachment to him was too great and the pain was more than she could bear. Daantje was three a half years old. He didn't want to go with us, but Nel talked him into it by promising that she would pick him up that evening. Of course, she did not come. Daantje sat by the front window in the dark, waiting for her until he fell asleep from exhaustion.

Daantje is fifty-eight at this writing. In spite of all of the scars we bear from that time, our family was blessed with his birth. For many years afterward, he would visit the family in s'Graveland during vacations. The house was a beautiful mansion on large lovely grounds with acres of lily-of-the-valley, his favorite flower to this day. Nel Vermey and her mother, Grandmother "Oma" Dinger, have since died. Daantje does not remember the war years, but he has wonderful memories of Oma's love and warmth during his subsequent visits. Nel's daughter lives in the United States and has made acquaintance with us, tied to our family by these remarkable circumstances.

Over the years we attempted to heal the pain that I had buried to help me survive. It created a difficult and distant relationship between Daantje and me. I could not revive my maternal feelings for him. Immediately after liberation, I got pregnant with our twin daughters. I hoped that having other children would trigger a re-attachment to my first child, but it did not happen that way. We consulted psychiatrists and a child specialist who examined Daantje several times and concluded that the boy was not really damaged because he was able to feel the love deeply buried in my heart. I tried, with help, to uncover my feelings, but after awhile the doctor and I decided it was better to let it rest. The past could not be undone. I had to live with the scars and by this time I had four more children to raise. Part of me could feel appreciative of the scars that reminded me of our survival. In the following years Daantje and I did fairly well together and our relationship improved over time. We now have a deep, loving respect for each other and a bond that unites us through the distant, indescribable past that we share. I have learned that where there is love, all things can heal.

Kees and I were fortunate to be able to rent the ground floor of a house in Utrecht belonging to a minister who had died during the last days of the war. His widow could not manage on the modest pension she received so she rented out part of the house. I was pregnant and felt very sick for the first couple of months. How well I remember walking to the store and stopping to throw up by every tree. They were beautiful, large chestnut trees and offered a strong trunk to grasp because I was so dizzy. The house was close to where my best friend, Plie lived. I went to see her often and she told me many stories of her life during the war. The following is the most impressive one.

Plie and her husband, Gerrit, ran a boarding house for students. She rented mainly to medical students, and being who she was, kept track of how far each person was in his studies and when the exams took place. It was a large, three-story house. Throughout the war years, she cooked three meals a day and served them in their rooms. Toward the end of the war, my uncle Eddie (the one who was "exempt" because of his non-Jewish wife) came to stay with Plie. He was actually hiding there because some of his friends in "mixed" marriages had been picked up by the Nazis. Plie and Gerrit had two children, but did not hesitate to take the risk of harboring Eddie. One day, friends warned them that the S.S. had been informed they were hiding a Jew. One of the boarders was a collaborator. Gerrit lifted up the planks in the living room floor and Eddie hid underneath. Within a half-hour, two S.S. men and a collaborator came ringing at the door. Gerrit let them in. They searched the house from top to bottom shouting out that they knew a Jew was hiding there. Plie and Gerrit kept their composure; Gerrit poured some coffee and started to read the paper. Plie went into the kitchen. The Nazis demanded to know where the Jew was. Plie calmly said, "You must be mistaken. There is no one like that here." The S.S. man said, "Oh, well we will see." They riddled the floor with bullets, shouting, "He's probably hiding under the floor!" Eddie was scared out of his mind, but he was not hit. Plie kept a composed countenance although her heart was pounding in her throat. The Nazis left. From then on, Plie and Gerrit knew there was an informer in the house. They never found out who it was.

Marie "Plie" Visscher in later years.

Gerrit died in the early 1980's. Plie passed away about five years later. She visited me in the United States several times and still lives in my memories. I went to her funeral with my uncle Eddie who was in his early eighties. He never ceased to be grateful for her heroic help during the war. None of us will ever stop being in debt to the righteous people who were true heroes.

Kees and I married on June 22, 1945. Over time, we found out what happened to family members. When we learned about the death camps and the torture in the concentration camps, we became even more appreciative of how fortunate we were to have escaped a worse fate than Westerbork.

Kees got a quasi-governmental job with a railroad maintenance factory in the southern village of Schijndel. There was a lot of work to be done throughout the country, repairing destroyed bridges and damaged railroad tracks. We were fortunate that he obtained employment quickly because after the war ended, Dutch currency was declared worthless and everyone was required to take their money to a bank where they were given a receipt that could be redeemed several days later for new currency. Kees was paid in the new money and this gave us the means to buy food. The factory sat next to a canal. There was no bridge, so we had to drive a long way to get to the nearest bridge in order to reach s'Hertogenbosch, the closest city.

Eline and Kees after the war.

Utrecht, 1947

We were given the use of a house that came with the job. We had to share it with another young couple, but we were so grateful to have it that we did not mind. It was a pleasant house in the little village of Schijndel, built out of red brick with shuttered windows and hardwood floors. The windows had been blown out by artillery fire, so kind friends gave us their picture-frame glass to replace what was broken. There were similar houses and farms nearby. I rode my bicycle into the village center to shop for flour, sugar and soap. I bought eggs, milk and bacon from the farms in the area, and grew vegetables. Our twin daughters, Juliet and Deborah, were born in 1946. So now, with our Daantje, we were a real family.

When we first moved into the Schijndel house, we had no electricity other than what was provided by the factory's generator that operated only during the day. At night we used candles and kerosene lamps. If I had enough wood or shavings, I cooked on the wood stove or on a kerosene burner. I learned to do the laundry by hand, putting white garments outside on the grass to bleach in the sun or draping them on wooden racks by the stove. In the winter, I hung diapers outside on a clothesline to dry. They froze and broke into pieces when I tried to fold them. I had a lot to learn.

Our war experience caused us to be apprehensive about staying in Europe. We wanted to move far away from Holland and the anti-Semitism that was still present. Maybe the monster would again raise its

Mietje and Daniel Dresden in better times after the war.

ugly face. We knew that life would never be as it was before. We decided to apply for immigration to the United States. We were told that the immigration quota was small and that it would take years before we would be able to go. We went on with our lives.

A couple of years later, I was about to give birth to our son, Cornelis. My husband was out of town. The doctor who had delivered the twins had retired. His replacement decided that there was plenty of time for him to eat dinner before coming to our house. A nurse had come to assist me, but at the crucial moment she was downstairs in the kitchen, doing the traditional boiling of water that one does in these situations. So, I delivered "Casey" myself because the doctor was late. The baby was blue, so I held him up by his feet and smacked him on his bottom to get him to breathe. It worked and everything went fine.

Two years later, my husband got a job in a plywood factory in Eindhoven and we moved to the big city. Here, our last child – a daughter, Eline – was born. Kees travelled to Rotterdam by train at night to attend school part-time and got a degree in engineering economics. He obtained employment with Philips, a large electronic concern. The children entered school, Kees' career went well and the years went by.

Daantje attended grade school in Eindhoven where he was taunted for being Jewish. Some of the students from his school beat him up on several occasions. At first he thought something was wrong with him and was extremely bewildered by the harassment. Kees and I told him there was nothing wrong with him, that it was the perpetrators who were wrong, and to not fight back in the hope that the attackers would lose interest and stop. In fact, that is what happened; but, as I contemplate what I would do today, I think I would give different advice. At the time, I believe I was still too frightened by the war to have recommended to my son to respond more assertively.

We were settled and did not think about our immigration application. One day, quite unexpectedly, we were notified that we had permission to immigrate. We had to decide quickly, otherwise, our names would go to the bottom of the list. We were in our thirties and our children's ages ranged from six to sixteen years; we knew it would be difficult to adjust to another country and culture. There were so many factors to consider and the future was impossible to predict. We wrote down the pros and cons of moving away and staying in Holland.

We couldn't decide. There had been political unrest in Hungary and this made us anxious. Fear of another war, good opportunities in my husband's field of work and our "gut" feelings tipped the scales. We decided to go.

We prepared the children for the move by having them listen to recordings of English language lessons every evening after dinner. They would fall asleep from boredom. We checked out Sears catalogs from the library to see what we could buy in the United States, since we were allowed to take only what we could fit into a crate measuring seven cubic meters. We took personal items and furnishings, including our bed frames, the few pieces of furniture that we reclaimed after the war, and the children's toys. We tried to immerse ourselves in a spirit of adventure. We took our camping tents, in the belief that we could live in them for a couple of months and save money. This turned out to be misguided, as we realized that living without an address would make job-hunting extremely difficult. It also proved to be a mistake to take our beds because American mattresses did not fit them. We had to have mattresses made, at great expense.

We considered moving to either Washington or Oregon, because of the good economy in the Northwest and the potential for technological growth in the area, and because the climate was similar to Holland – not too hot in the summer. We finally decided on Oregon because my brother, Tony, lived there.

In 1958, we made the move. We rented a house and Kees found a job within three months. The children picked berries in the summer to make extra money. I used the money to buy school clothes for them. They were proud to contribute to the family budget with their hard earned wages; as a reward, we would all go to the drive-in theatre on Saturday night for one dollar per car. Daantje, now going by "Daniel," was a teenager and had the most difficult time with the change. He enlisted in the Marines at the age of nineteen where he again experienced anti-Semitic prejudice, including physical attacks, from fellow soldiers and a drill sergeant. As a young adult, he returned to Holland to visit whenever he could afford the trip and it took many years before he felt that he came "home" when he returned to the United States.

We bought a house with five acres in a rural area near Portland. The house did not have heat or a municipal water supply and needed a lot of repairs. We managed to fix it up into an attractive home and kept horses and chickens on the property. It was a good, comfortable life. Kees did well in his profession and I took care of the house and children, working at temporary jobs to make money for birthday gifts and other extras. The older children married and established their own families and careers. Then Kees left us.

Some well-meaning friends tried to comfort me by saying that if I could survive the war I could survive anything. I thought, however, that it was easier to bear the suffering at the hands of an enemy than to be abandoned by the person I thought of as my partner for life. But, I had to go on. I returned to school and got a job as an engineering technician. Years later I got licensed as a professional land surveyor. I am still haunted by some of my war experiences, but I firmly believe that my ability to retain hope has served me well in times of pain and adversity.

* * * * * *

In the fall of 1999, Daniel (or Daantje) returned to Holland with his wife, Faith, to participate in a memorial ceremony in honor of his war mother, Nel, who had passed away several years before. Cultural Attaché of the Embassy of Israel, Ilan Fluss, presented a commemorative medal to Nel's daughter, Marcia. Daniel was fifty-seven years old. In his speech, he said:

"During a horrible time in the world, I had two loving mothers, both heroes – Eline, who had the courage to separate from me, and Nel, who had the courage to risk her life to adopt me."

For many years I had wanted to go to Israel to pay respect to the relatives I had lost in the war, particularly my maternal grandparents. My retirement in 1993 afforded me the opportunity to do so. I went with a group of volunteers and was assigned to the geriatric unit of a large hospital next to an army base in Tel A Shamir, twenty miles from Tel Aviv. I felt ill prepared because I did not speak Hebrew or Polish and the patients did not speak English. I had to figure out what the patient wanted; was it tea or coffee or maybe chocolate? Through trial and error, we eventually achieved mutual understanding. Strong tea with lots of milk and sugar? Okay, that I could do.

Sometimes I had to feed very old and frail patients. They seemed lonely and grateful for the attention. Many of them had escaped from somewhere during the war and had no relatives in Israel. They looked sad during visiting hours, so I tried to comfort them. It felt good to be of help even though I often felt sad myself. Some of them had been young when they came to Israel and had raised families there. Their relatives would come to visit or take them home for an afternoon. It was a difficult assignment but it helped me to make peace with some of my past. I felt so appreciative when I came home and was greeted at the airport by my children and grandchildren. I would like to go with them to Israel one day to see the country and its daily struggle for existence and its many colorful people.

I also visited the Masada, the site of the last resistance against the Romans. Here, the Jews were ultimately unable to defend themselves and all committed suicide. From this place, one can see Libya and Egypt to the south, Jordan to the east, Iraq to the north, and, on a clear day, in your minds eye, Auschwitz to the northwest.

I never felt afraid in Israel even though there were terrorist attacks on buses and soldiers with machine guns everywhere. This time I knew they were there to protect me, not to persecute or imprison me. I went to Yad Vashem, the Holocaust Memorial, where records are kept in a vast library. The death books are ledger-sized and contain the names of my grandparents, my uncle and my aunt. I saw the name of my husband's uncle and aunt, neatly typed with the dates of their birth and date and place of death. My grandparents were gassed on the day of their arrival at Auschwitz, just a few days after they left Holland. I think they died together, as I am told that men and women were not separated in the gas chambers. I hope they did not suffer long. My heart breaks when I remember their hopeful postcard, trying to convince themselves and us that they had useful skills that might save their lives. I will always remember them, and through this recollection, I hope to memorialize them for all time.

The memorial at Yad Vashem, the Holocaust Museum in Jerusalem which houses the Death Books containing the names of individuals killed in the concentration camps. The six torches represent the six million people who died.

EPILOGUE

Throughout the history of mankind, catastrophes have occurred. There have been natural disasters, wars, disease, epidemics, and there have been periods of mass persecution that were conducted in the name of religion. The effects of these events on the lives of the survivors has not often been described in history books. After World War II and the Holocaust, the medical profession began to pay attention to the phenomenon that is now often referred to as "Post-Traumatic Stress Disorder." It includes a number of symptoms experienced by individuals who have experienced a catastrophic event. In severe cases, the victims are not able to work to sustain themselves, to cope effectively with their distress or to lead fulfilling lives. Sometimes families are broken apart as psychological symptoms and painful emotions cause great difficulty and disruption.

I was fortunate to have not been disabled by my experiences during the war. I believe I was blessed with a constitutional strength that, along with a loving family, helped me endure the after-effects of the war. As a final word to this chronicle, I wish to describe some of the psychological and emotional difficulties I have experienced because of what I lived through.

After my husband left me, I had to develop a career and find a job. This was when certain symptoms began to emerge that were frightening to me. I chose to get more education, but, approaching the age of fifty, decided not to pursue a medical degree, which had been my original goal as a young woman. So, I worked part-time and obtained an Associate degree in engineering. My youngest child was still living at home and had to quit college. She went to live with one of my older daughters for awhile. I found employment with the government, and heeding the advice of my oldest son, learned the profession of land surveying. At the time I was working with an all-men crew. I was well aware that I had entered a male profession and that I would face some difficulties. While many of my co-workers were quite nice, there was one young man on the crew who treated me terribly. Many times I had to work alone with him. It was hard work, often involving physical labor, and he deliberately made it more difficult. He would send me ahead through brush and bramble to clear a path, and when I had done so, he would call me back to fetch gasoline for his chain saw. Being low on the hierarchy, I had to carry all of the tools and equipment. He seemed to take pleasure in placing hardship on me. One autumn day in eastern Washington, we had to walk a long distance through a wheat field to set a survey monument to mark the spot for a power-line tower. It involved the digging of a deep hole in which to secure a long pipe with a brass cap on one end. He leaned against a fence, lit a cigarette, and said, "Dig." I started to dig the half-frozen earth. He smiled and said, "Faster." This went on until the hole was done. I did not want to give him the satisfaction of seeing me cry. He kept up this kind of treatment until we returned to our truck to go home. I saw him grinning as I got in.

From that day on, I would often wake up in the middle of the night with the sensation of choking. I could not breathe. Terrified, I came close to fainting. I went to the doctor who conducted many tests and finally concluded that I was experiencing panic attacks. I was told that if I fainted, my tensions would release and I would regain consciousness. To me, it was clear that I associated the young man's treatment of me with the Nazi guards in the camp, and their yelling, their cruel smiles and their obvious enjoyment in watching the inmates suffer and cower in fear. I don't have the panic attacks as frequently as I once did and medication has helped, but they still occur without warning.

Some years later, with study and experience under my belt, I was ready to take the state examination for land surveyors. I knew the material, but at the exam, I froze and failed. I was terribly discouraged. Six months later, I tried it again, but experienced the same problem: I broke out in a sweat and could barely breathe. Once more I failed. I had never experienced fright over exams before and I could not understand it. On the advice of a friend, I went to see a psychologist. After the third visit, I realized that the exam proctor, who paced about the room and would walk up behind my chair, wore black boots like the ones worn by the S.S. officers. The next time I took the test, I passed!

I know that I am fortunate to have survived the years of fright and misery in a way that allows me to be productive and to enjoy life. I do not underestimate the support I get from the love of my children and grandchildren, and the pleasure I get from my great-grandchildren. Certainly, the survivors of any major hardship will find strength in those things. So many other people, however, are scarred for life.

Cruelty, genocide and oppression of whole peoples still exist in the world today. I believe we can all do something to stop these evils, in our hometowns, in our organizations, at work. We must also take care of ourselves and each other in order to survive whatever may come in these difficult times. And most of all, we must make our young people understand the critical importance of accepting the differences of others and help them to be aware of the dangers of ignorance and submission, which are often hidden in disguise.

* * * * * *

ABOUT THE AUTHOR

Eline Hoekstra Dresden was born in The Hague, The Netherlands, in 1923. She was detained in the Dutch transit camp, Westerbork, for almost three years during World War II. She moved to the United States with her husband and five children in 1958, and settled in Oregon City, Oregon, near Portland where she worked for many years as a land surveyor for the Army Corps of Engineers. Prompted by recent neo-Nazi movements in the U.S. and Europe, by growing denial of the Holocaust, and by "ethnic cleansing" operations in central Europe and Africa, she speaks to students of all ages about her experiences during World War II and about the dangers of prejudice. She has compiled her memories in the manuscript, *Wishing Upon A Star*. Her "Letter to My Children" is published in the compilation, *Letters to Our Daughters*, edited by Kristine Van Raden and Molly Davis, published in 1999, by Hyperion. In 1998, an interview about her war experience was preserved on videotape (No. 47981) and added to the collection of The Shoah Visual History Foundation, created by film director, Steven Spielberg.

ABOUT THE PUBLISHER'S LOGO

As my four-year old great granddaughter played with the pendant on my necklace, rolling its small metal balls around in their cage (this is a part of a thrust bearing) she asked, "Big Grandma, is this the only necklace you have?" My children and their children had all played with this pendant, a metal ring with its twelve little freeturning balls placed like numbers on a clock. My answer to her was, "No, but this is my favorite one and it is the only one I wear." When she grows up I hope to tell her this story:

"Many years ago there was a long terrible war. I was a prisoner in a horrible place for several years with many other people. All of the prisoners had to work hard. Some of them were ordered to salvage parts of American planes that had been brought down, including B-17 bombers and Mustang fighters. They stripped the airplanes of their heavy copper wires, colored electrical wires and bearings. All these materials were re-used by our captors, the Nazis. Finally, the war ended and I was freed from the nightmare of that place. On my last day there, as I was leaving I grabbed a handful of bearings I saw piled nearby. I hung one from a string and put it around my neck as a good luck charm. I have worn it ever since then, exchanging the string for a gold chain. Over the years it took on a great meaning for me... a reminder to stay on a true bearing in my life."

The following essay was written by Nel Vermey's granddaughter, Juliana Carlson. It was the winning essay in the 3rd and 4th Grade Age Group for the South Orange Maplewood 22nd Annual Interfaith Holocaust Remembrance Service, held April 13, 1999.

A PREJUDICE ESSAY

by Juliana Carlson
Grade 4, Tuscan School
Maplewood, New Jersey

Imagine having a Nazi soldier knock on the door to take you away to a work camp because you hid a Jewish baby. Imagine being taken away from your home against your will. I happen to be lucky enough to have a grandmother who risked that consequence by hiding a Jewish baby in Holland during the war.

She isn't alive, that brave woman. I never met her, because she died before I was born, but I know one thing. Her story is a very important one, and it's a story that just recently added a happy ending.

Let me start from one person's point of view: Eline Hoekstra had a newborn baby. This baby was Daniel. Unfortunately for Daniel and his family, he was born in a very hard time. The Holocaust. Eline was Jewish and her husband was half-Jewish. They knew the dangers of keeping their baby, yet they did not want to part. They were sure of one good thing, though. Daniel was a lucky baby in some ways. He had blond hair and blue eyes, which could help him pass for a non-Jewish baby. Eline spoke to a friend who was friends with my Oma, my grandmother. She wasn't nearly my Oma yet, and she was pretty fresh and young. She had been parted from my Opa, my grandfather (not nearly my Opa yet), as he was off in America. She knew that there were terrible dangers, but she decided to take care of Daniel.

Right now is where I think she acted the bravest. Despite the chances of being caught, she decided to take this risk to save Daniel, a risk that I now look up to with great pride. As soon as Eline and her husband had given up the baby, they went into hiding. Not knowing who my Oma, Louise Vermey was, was a great risk for them, but my Oma took great pride in caring for Daniel. She knit sweaters and jackets for him and watched him grow up. She was a physical therapist and was allowed to have a bicycle, so she could get things the family needed. Her family also had a "forbidden" radio, so she knew all that was going on.

After the war, Eline came back. She was dreading taking Daniel away, but everyone knew she was his rightful mother. It was sadly agreed by all that Daniel should not be allowed to see my Oma again, but he was allowed to see my great-Oma. This was a treat to Daniel, and every summer he did just that.

Now that Daniel is an adult, he has a better relationship with his mother. My Oma and great-Oma have passed away, and many other changes have taken place. I understand her painful story as one that I will pass on to younger children who will pass it on as well.

While I was on vacation in February, my mother got the most important call I have ever witnessed. After she hung up the phone, she came over to me. She talked about how for so long Eline had been trying to get my Oma's name added to the List of the Righteous in Israel. The phone call was from Eline saying that it had happened. Louise Vermey's name, and her parents' names will be added on the Righteous Honor Wall at Yad Vashem in Israel.

BIBLIOGRAPHY

Dresden, Daniel. *De Beul Regeert (The Hatchet Man Rules)*. The Hague, The Netherlands: Hofstad, 1945.

Dresden, Sem. *Persecution, Extermination, Literature.* Toronto Press, 1995.

United States Holocaust Museum. *Historical Atlas of the Holocaust.* United States Holocaust Museum, Washington, D.C. New York: Macmillan Publishing USA; Simon and Schuster Macmillan, 1996.

Yahill, Lenie. *The Holocaust: The Fate of European Jewry*. Oxford University Press, 1990.

RECOMMENDED READING

Buchwalter, Marianne. *Memories of a Berlin Childhood.* Corvallis, Oregon: Premier Editions International Inc., 1995.

Hillesum, Etty. *Het Verstoorde Leven*. Amsterdam: Balans Publishers, 1993.

Kern, Alice. *Tapestry of Hope*. United States, 1988.

Miller, Melissa ed. *The Diary of Anne Frank*. New York: Metropolitan Books, Henry Holt and Co., 1998 revised.

Spiegelman, Art. *Maus: A Survivor's Tale*. New York: Pantheon Books, 1986.

Wiesel, Elie. *Memoirs, All Rivers Run to the Sea.* New York, Alfred A. Knopf, 1996.